C000144835

I dedicate this book with lots of love to my husband, my children and their families, to all those who motivated me to write it and to all those who read it; I have written this book for you.

CONTENTS

· ·

CONTENTS (CONTINUED)

INTRODUCTION

I have found many beautiful and loving people who were not aware that we can make life more enjoyable through the knowledge of who we really are. Talking about life in general, I would say how I see it and they would be surprised. Some of them were somehow shocked. They seemed pleased to hear it, but at the same time they had doubts. They could not quite believe it. It was contradictory to what they had been brought up with and they found it difficult to believe. Some of them would say, "It sounds good but I have never heard anything like this before". I could detect fear and when I asked them if they felt it, they said "yes". I very much hope that this book will encourage readers to look into themselves, to be curious and start practising techniques, using tools to help themselves and looking for more information, especially within themselves. There are treasures hidden under many layers of our exterior life. Unless we search for them we will not fully benefit from them.

When I set out to write this book, I was not sure where to start or what to say. What I knew was that it had to be written. Awakening is so important. I got ready to start and waited patiently. I use "we" in most of the book, because although I wrote it, the content came from my other me, so the two of us were one.

This is a book without a beginning or an end. It is just for whatever moment in life you happen to be in. Open it at random and the page will be exactly what you need to draw your attention. It is a book that invites you to go deeper within and reflect on how your life is or could be. It invites you to see if there are changes you can make or options you can choose. Each topic has something to tell the reader and each requires some time to ponder over it.

Different people use words in different ways. To avoid confusion, here is what I mean by the following words. "Whole" or "collective" express all living creation on the planet. "Source" refers to the source of all creation.

DESCRIPTION OF THE BOOK

This book will help those who are ready to wake up, those who are waking up, those who are awake but forget it at times, and anyone who wants to be reminded that our life is more than what it seems to be.

It is a book that touches on subjects of our every day life with just a page or so on each subject. However, each subject requires time and reflection after the topic has been read in order to benefit from it more fully.

It is not a book to read and put aside. It is to be kept to hand and opened any time at random, or you could go through the index and find the topic that suits the moment you are in.

RESISTANCES

• •

Are we aware of our resistances? If we are, how often do we catch them interfering in our lives? Have you noticed how subtle they are in settling in? All the time we carry on as if they were not there, ignoring the symptoms they may cause. How about if we stopped and asked ourselves the whys and why nots of not doing those things we love doing? Our dreams - are we working towards achieving them? In order to find out, we can take a few minutes, close our eyes and check if we are doing everything that our heart is longing for, if we are satisfied that our dreams and wishes have been met and dealt with. We could make a list and then proceed to check it out, starting with those things which are most important to us. It could be a trip we want to make that has not happened yet, learning to play the guitar or learning a language, writing a book, founding a charity, becoming a doctor or being a guide.

Once the list has been made, we take one item from it. We examine it and leave it in our minds with silent questions: "Why has this not happened? What has stopped it or what is stopping it?" Then, we wait in silence and let the answers come to us. We will not have to wait long. These answers have been waiting for us for a long time. They have been waiting for us to notice that something was not quite right and they want to come to the surface and show us what has been hidden from us. As the answers come out, all the excuses we were making for our desire not to take place will vanish and give way to the real reason. There was a resistance stopping us from doing what we wanted to do. The resistance was there because there was a feeling, a strong feeling, causing it. A lot of the time it is fear, but it could be something else. Usually it is a negative feeling that creates the resistance.

Having found what was creating the resistance, you would proceed to remove it with a silent and non-judgemental mind by looking for its location in the body. Some people will find it in a particular part of the physical body, others will feel it all over and others will feel it in the head. There are those who will not feel any particular sensation in the body. Having found the energy, talk to it and welcome it, giving it time to come out and expand. Encourage it to grow to its maximum. Some will feel the energy expanding and when it stops expanding, go to your heart and with your unconditional love, surround it and send it to Source. As you are talking to these blockages of energy you are telling them exactly what you are doing. If you cannot feel the blockages of energy, you can still do it as if you were feeling them. The results will be the same, and when it is done you will feel a pleasing sensation of wellbeing and liberation. When the process has finished, check it again and see if it has gone or if there are still bits left. Or maybe some of it has gone to a different part of the body. If that is the case, do the process again. If you are dealing with a heavy case or with one which has many layers, you may have to do it more than once. But that is fine. It will go with perseverance.

When you have dealt with the first item on your list, then keep working with the rest. It is a good idea to take it in a relaxed manner and do one a day until the list is finished. Afterwards, it is a question of keeping resistances in check. It is important to remember, as you unblock those resistances which were stopping you from doing what you wanted, to go ahead and do them, and enjoy what had been your wish all along.

FEELING LOST

· ·

How many times have you felt lost, in the sense that you do not know what to do? When there is a feeling of impotence and you are in an emptiness that wants to swallow you into the deepest hole? When inertia seems to take over and all our senses are paralysed and we cannot move to save ourselves?

In order to avoid getting into that situation, it is important to bear in mind who we are. We are infinite and limitless. Our higher Self is with us at all times, whether we feel it or not. We are being taken care of constantly, at every minute of our lives. That reassurance gives us solace and security so we can keep our control, no matter what. We easily forget who we are by taking this physical world for our reality when it is only a projection, where we are projected for a period of time to experience or learn things we are curious about.

I do not know about you. For me, the first time I felt lost was as a baby. I felt cold and uncomfortable. I could not move because my parents had wrapped me up so tight with clothes that I thought I was going to suffocate. What was worse, I could not speak yet, so I could not communicate or control the situation. My most poignant experiences of feeling lost include when I was four years old and my father died. Another one was when I was on night duty as a Samaritan, in London. In the middle of the night, a 12 year old girl rang and pleaded with me to help her parents to get back together. Her words held so much hope and belief that I could do it that I felt completely lost. I had no words to explain to the child that it was not in my hands. No matter what I said, she came up with words to tell me that if I talked to them they would see things the way she did. I felt so very lost. My heart was breaking into pieces and I wanted a magic wand to make it happen for her. Another experience was when I visited Brixton prison in London as a Samaritan. As I was walking down a corridor, a prisoner behind bars called out to me and asked me to pray with him. It was not what he asked, which I gladly gave him; it was how he felt that made me feel lost.

Through the passing years, I have witnessed many situations where there is a big ocean of emptiness and desolation in which it is easy to be lost. I have also learned that we are all connected and that I feel what the people involved are feeling. In my awareness of who we are, I soon became able to be calm and pass that energy on to people who asked for help so that they would also be calm.

There are many situations in our everyday life when we can feel lost. How about if we looked around us? All those people moving about are part of us. We are connected. The whole creation on earth is connected. There is no space to be lost because we are one big mass of energy with different forms. We are not lost, we are where we are supposed to be at all times; and the most amazing thing is that we chose to be wherever we are. We chose every situation we experience, even though it is hard to admit we would have done that to ourselves. Yet we have.

Are you prepared to look around and enhance the magnitude of what surrounds us? Being lost is not knowing ourselves. Making excuses is not taking responsibility. It is not wanting to learn the lesson, because it is easier to be miserable in the known than happy in the unknown. Moving forward to the unknown is like waking up to a new morning. Meeting the new day with a smile, fresh enthusiasm and ready to learn and move on is the key. There are no barriers we cannot break down. There are no obstacles we cannot dissolve. There are no difficulties we cannot overcome. In fact, there is nothing that can get in our way, if we have the right disposition and we know who we are and what we want to get out of life. For me it is to be happy and contribute to the happiness and awakening of others.

BELIEVING

. . . .

Believing in ourselves is the most powerful thing we can do. Believing that we are supreme powers even if we are not aware of the magnitude of it. By just believing it, it will manifest itself every time we need it. In my experience, when I look outside myself for answers, they never come in neat packages. There are always things missing, blockages, emptiness with no sense, void corners, exaggerations or shortness. In other words, I may see a reflection of what I am looking for but never the real thing, never what I want to find. Of course not, because the answers are within myself, clear and simple, and when I find them they fit perfectly. Given time, all the questions come into the light with the most enlightening answers.

Reaching this stage of our lives is a great accomplishment, because from here on, all situations seem to have a sequential trail. Following the trail will take us where we want to be, even though we have no idea where that might be as we are moving on. We can see it like in a game. Like those games children love playing. This is so similar to those games. As a consequence of beliefs, intentions and movements the games evolve and get to wherever they get. This life of ours, on the planet, does not seem to be any different. Although here, we have to know the rules well. At least, be humble enough and allow for those rules of the game to be explained to us; in a way we can understand easily, so we do not over-complicate things. Being humble and acknowledging that we only know what we are supposed to know will be of great help for us to move on.

The first thing for us to understand is that we created a game and then we activated it. This is where we come in. In passing through this physical form we are living the projection of our game. We could say we are playing our game, our creation or projection. Our confusion comes from having forgotten what happened before we arrived on the planet and from meeting other beings who have also forgotten it. However, for those who seek it, the solution is not far away. In fact, it is within us. When the game is not fun and becomes distorted, because it has been taken seriously, it is then that the problems start in our lives. Here we encounter blockages of ignorance of who we are and what we came to do. The search starts and it takes many forms, shapes and ideologies, and there are many people who follow them. From this, leaders, gurus, teachers come up and they all preach to the masses, wanting to be believed and followed.

The AWAKENING is necessary now: awakening to who we are and what we are doing in this "now". The simplest way I know to do this is to go within and listen carefully in silence. Give it time. Make time for this silent listening every day. This is how we will hear the answers, which are waiting for us to allow them to be expressed. It is such a relief! Such joy! Such wellbeing at having realised where our true Self is and how easily we can contact it! In fact, we are in contact all the time because it has never left us. It is the original project maker, who projected the whole game. We were given full control to play the game and we lost ourselves in the game, forgetting who we are and the fact that we are only playing a game.

We can see what games do to people. Football fans lose themselves in fanatical behaviour. They can be ill or have a heart attack due to the emotions from the game. Other sports have the same effect on other people. Card games have ruined families. It is interesting to observe how humans keep inventing more and more games to play and yet they forget the one they came to play. Could it be that they lost themselves in the original game and that they keep looking for new ones to compensate for it?

THERE IS ONE THING WE SHOULD KNOW

We carry with us all the knowledge we could ever want to have. However, we think the opposite. We tend to think we do not know and that we have to study a lot, have lots of teachers and go to lots of schools or universities. Imagine that we went into a huge library with thousands of books; with masses of information about everything possible we wished to know. Imagine that with a sweep of the head through the books, we would have all that information at our disposal. Imagine that then we would know everything there is to know. Then, what? What would happen? If we knew everything there is to know there would be no more to do. What do you think?

Knowing everything makes us God. Here is the irony. Who believes he or she is God? And yet, that is what we are. We are cells of the Universal Intelligence, mini universes with all the qualities of the matrix, the mother base. So, we are all mini Gods. All we have to do is remember this and allow ourselves to be guided by that part of us; allow it to be our satellite navigation to make sure we do not lose our way and instead go straight to the objectives we came to achieve. Doing that we would not have the problems and chaos we have. Neither would we have the wars.

So, who are we? What are we doing? Why do so many of us want to come to this planet?

We are projections of the Universal Light, programmed to achieve certain tasks in a specific time. If we forget who we are and get lost, we somehow change the project and it could become longer or shorter. We need to explore and learn to go back to our project. We create our own difficulties by not being in our centre. From that, we can get directions as to what to do and how to go about whatever tasks we have in hand. The possibilities can be many and it is up to us to choose the right ones. So we are given plenty of freedom to use initiative and expansion. That can work beautifully well, if we project from within our hearts and remember who we are. However, if we project from our intellect and become a "know it all" and "know it best"; then, we are doomed. We are like magnets and we attract what we think and feel.

We have multiple battles with ourselves and with the world. One thing to remember is that it all starts with ourselves, even though we blame others or our circumstances merely because that is the easy way of not having to remember who we are. There seems to be a fear of knowing who we are. I have met many people who have deep problems that could be solved really easily but they do not want to go inside themselves. If pushed a little, there is fear in their eyes and their whole body tenses as if something terrible were going to happen. Those people are stuck or caught in blockages of energy created by themselves and they find it difficult to move away from the blockages. When someone wants to help them, they behave as if they wanted to hide away, even though they want very much to be helped. Then, they feel worse because they want help and at the same time they are not able to accept it. They are in a vicious cycle, which keeps them enclosed in fear.

Being open and, with the innocence of a child, being trusting as a child trusts its mother, allowing for help to reach us and when it is there accepting it, would put many people on their way to recovering their power. Being silent and allowing our inner voice to be heard, trusting it, believing it, appreciating it and being grateful that it is there for us, will lead us back to our natural path.

ILLUSIONARY POWER

• •

Some people want to control the world using violence and cruelty. They want power and they think that by abusing human rights they have it. They are the ones who inflict horrendous laws on others and make those under them enforce their laws. Then, there are the people who want to benefit from them, ignoring that they are contributing and helping those fanatics to increase the horror in the world.

Our planet is a benevolent planet: generous, giving, loving, beautiful. So where do these heartless beings come from? Did someone implant them here on earth as an infectious plague? What do they want? What for? Do they realise that all their power is useless if the earth wants to shake them out of existence with a natural disaster? They may think they are invincible with all the destructive equipment they posses. However, the earth can put all that to no use with a simple shake, a tsunami or a hurricane. They believe their illusions are the real thing, forgetting they are unreal projections and the matrix can stop them at any time.

What is there for us to do? What is our role in all that? How can we be instruments of help? And what would our purpose be? Fighting them with the same weapons is a dead end. Judging them or using another type of force would be equally ineffective. We have to wake up to who we really are and know what to do. How can we deal with these situations as individuals in a way that clears the darkness and brings the light? The main thing would be to ask ourselves relevant questions, which could help us to be of assistance to others and ourselves, because as we help others we are helping ourselves and as we destroy others we destroy ourselves too.

When witnessing distressful incidents or hearing about them, instead of fuming with rage, wanting to retaliate or judging the perpetrators, it would be more helpful to use our inner power of peace, love and joy to calm the waves of darkness of those places and people. It is important not to forget who we are, where we came from and what our mission is supposed to achieve in this present projection we are in. Bearing in mind all those things, we can go forward guided as to what to do, when and where: our heart at peace, our mind calm, our actions precise and the results helpful.

Meanwhile, being diligent and good humoured, joyful and helpful, giving a hand wherever needed and being available to assist, grateful for what we have, thankful to all around us, that is what we are able to do on a daily basis to comply with our humanity on earth, always bearing in mind how sacred our planet and its creation are and how dependant we are on it whilst in our physical bodies. Also, we can remember that every single bit of creation on the planet has its role to play and is equally important to the harmony and wellbeing of the whole. The fact that those who have not been awakened yet cannot see it does not mean that it is not so.

Let us not waste time concentrating our attention on news which is distressing and which we cannot deal with in a practical and physical way. Let us instead get stronger in our resolution to help by going within and working from that place we know best, bringing the best out in everyone, everything and everywhere. Let us be strong and join forces with those who are like-minded. Let us reassure ourselves that we are loved and helped with every step we take and that we are watched and guided, if we allow it. Let us join the collective in our pursuit of the higher good for all on our planet and beyond. Let us be the Light we are. Let our Light dissolve any fear around us and in the whole world. So be it.

WHERE DO WE STAND IN RELATION TO OTHERS?

Human beings suffer because of others in many ways. One of them is when we impose pain on ourselves. Parents suffer and worry about their children, no matter what age they are. The children become parents themselves and suffer for their children and their parents, especially when these are elderly or ill. Children also suffer because they have been with that energy around them since they were born. We also extend our suffering to relatives, friends, neighbours and anyone reported on the news that has been hurt, misbehaved or whatever, according to our criteria of seeing the world.

We would be in a better situation if we asked ourselves some simple questions, such as: Why am I worrying? Who do I help by suffering? What is the benefit of it? Am I changing people or situations for the better with my worrying and suffering? What really happens when I spread this negative energy around me? Who gets hurt? How does it affect me? How does it affect my surroundings, those around me, the whole planet?

The answers to those questions will clearly define what we are doing. How do we remove ourselves from that pattern, which we have learned from our ancestors? We carry it from generation to generation. We adjust to it as something normal, because most people do. It is a well-known thing to do. It is a habit inherited from our ancestors and we carry on with it without questioning it. We are not aware of the consequences that these feelings can have. We do not do this consciously; therefore, we do not know what we are doing. However, if we were to ask any one of these individuals the reasons for their suffering, they would go into great detail in their explanation with a certainty of being right. When looking from an awareness of understanding we can see how tied up people are without realising it. To separate our ties needs knowledge and a will to do so. It needs an awakening call in the mind and liberation of the heart. It is important to be honest with ourselves, have the courage to face it, do something about it and get help to make a start and guide our first steps. Wanting to learn and having an inquisitive mind will help the progress a great deal.

Guilt is one of the most common feelings that comes up when dealing with situations of wanting to move away from what is discussed above. Guilt is a strong negative energy, which can undermine any good intention of putting the situation in its place for the wellbeing of all. When guilt hits home, there is an ill feeling about what we do in our lives. There is insecurity in us. We doubt ourselves. We lose the notion of what is the right thing or not, but we cannot discuss it with anyone because this feeling makes us feel ashamed of ourselves. So we are caught in a spider's web. We want to get out but how do we get out without being caught? If only we could appease our mind for a while, entering into silence and reflexion, we would be touching our real Self within, telling ourselves what is best for us in relation to the others we worry about or suffer for. We would see a sparkling light showing us the way, what to do, who to approach and the steps to take in order to find ourselves. We would find ourselves free from suffering or worrying, because we would know and understand that we have to make decisions that affect us and are good for us, and that others have to do exactly the same. Knowing that we all have the same possibilities to do well and that nobody can direct our way but ourselves will lead us onto the path of success and wellbeing, not only for us but also for the whole world. Not having some knowledge of who our true Self is can be somewhat disconcerting for us, but some knowledge can take us a long way towards freedom and where we want to be.

INFLUENCES - 1 -

. . . .

Even though we think we are strong in our beliefs and that no one can shake them, we may be surprised at how easily, without being aware, we fall into the trap of agreeing with someone about a subject we have not discussed. We can be caught by a simple word or sentence that means a lot to us, and we can hang onto those words without going any further to see the real meaning of what we have been given to understand. If someone were to point out to us the consequences of our actions, we would be shocked at how unaware we had been caught. It is so easy to be influenced by the masses because they carry strong energy due to the number of them taking part in their cry for what they want, which is not always what everyone wants, the best for humankind or for the planet.

Being aware is so very important in order not to fall into pits that we do not know anything about. Being in the present in full awareness pays off not only for us to be safe but also to contribute to the wellbeing of the whole. So does asking ourselves questions before we get involved in matters which could be damaging to everyone. What is all this about? Do I know or understand it? How can my involvement in it help in any way? Who are the beneficiaries of all this? Who suffers from all this? By answering our questions we will get to our present moment and our awareness of being connected to our true Self, which will be able to guide us in what to do in that situation.

Some people can be confused. They talk about freedom without knowing what freedom is. They look for freedom outside themselves and expect others to give it to them. For that alone they can go to war. They can convince millions, through mere power, to get what they want, which is not freedom but the power to control others. We must have a very clear understanding that nobody can give us freedom but ourselves. The freedom that brings peace is in the mind. If our mind is not at peace, we do not have freedom.

Those who are looking for freedom outside themselves are wasting their precious time on earth, forgetting that they are passengers with a limited time in their passport that allows them to be on the planet. They are forgetting that they are very temporary and can be gone at any minute. They are forgetting that they already have everything they are fighting for. They are also forgetting what their purpose in life is. So why follow them? Why believe them? What are they going to give you that you do not already have? Do you realise that by following them you are denying yourself? You become the doer of their ideas, while yours are buried somewhere unknown to you. This is a time for reflexion. Your original purpose in life was not to run after someone else's ideas. Reflect on this.

Victorious heroes are those who, through their own power, achieve great deeds without shouting or screaming, without preaching or convincing, without creating victims or oppressors and without harming the atmosphere with their influences. Their very presence is enough to make you feel humble and at peace. They do not have to speak to be heard. They emanate freely and easily that which those in their ignorance are looking for. They are the heroes that show us the way of being without hurting anyone, while bringing harmony and calm into a society lacking these things. We could all be those heroes. If we looked inside ourselves for guidance and allowed ourselves moments of silence and reflection, freedom and peace would be within our reach.

INFLUENCES - 2 -

· ·

We are influenced constantly by everything around us, even the things we do not want to be influenced by. These still manage to filter into our lives as they present themselves as something we do not want. They are in our presence when we say, "we do not want them to be part of us".

We are influenced at the moment of being born by the way we are welcomed into the physical world. Our parents play a big role in influencing us by the way they bring us up, as do teachers, friends and every contact we have in this physical world. It could be animals or anything, such as rocks or cars. Of course, the internet is the biggest influence now for most people, and that can be an advantage or disadvantage depending on how we allow ourselves to be influenced. Awareness is of great importance. If we are aware, we are in a position to take decisions and allow or disallow whatever is happening at any given moment.

The influences we are exposed to through our childhood and adolescence mark our lives. Many times there are opportunities to change them around, but we do not always take those opportunities and sometimes as a result we end up with disastrous consequences.

In adulthood we load ourselves with responsibilities of all kinds and the influences we find ourselves surrounded with have increased to such a high level that many people cannot deal with them. They may have depressions, illnesses or other problems, reflecting how they have been affected by the influences they have been exposed to.

There are different ways of being influenced:

- We can follow others and give them our power, so we are totally dedicated to those people we consider superior to us, or we feel a duty towards them, therefore missing our opportunities to evolve.
- We can follow others and take from them only those ideas that suit and resonate within us, thus retaining our power.
- We can listen to what others have to say, and tap into our inner wisdom to know which way will be the best for us to take.

By interfering with other people's ways of life, we are not helping. We are getting in their way, preventing them from doing what they came to do. However, we could be the ones who help them by putting obstacles in their way, creating problems for them to solve. There is a very fine line between the two and it is important for us to differentiate them. Removing lifetime habits of interfering can prove challenging, but the benefit will be for both parties.

Our level of energies will put us in different dimensions of existence. This will affect our relationship with others considerably, because we see life from different angles and levels. Discomfort may occur in relationships. What should we do? It will be a question of adjusting on both sides, but mainly on the side of those who can understand the process that is taking place. This will be done without interfering in other people's lives. Influences come and go. It is up to us what we do with them.

THE JIGSAW

· ·

I, personally, find it puzzling how we are finding the missing pieces in our lives and how we build up the whole picture. For some it is quick and for others it is slow. Sometimes the discovery of a new piece can make one euphoric with enthusiasm and satisfaction, and other times, when one feels the vacuum and the missing piece is not in sight, it can be discouraging. However, with patience and the trust that we will find it, we carry on with our lives, allowing the circumstances of life to bring to us the opportunity to keep finding those missing pieces that can make the whole picture visible.

Although we are all part of the same energy, we are so uniquely different that our ways of finding those missing pieces are diverse, according to our knowledge on the subject we are dealing with. When we have a strong intent to know who we really are and why this and that is happening to us, it is then we ask ourselves questions to find the answers. We find that extremely exciting and we want more of it, so we get onto a path that promises results. We become the path. We become the discovery. We become the missing pieces. We become the actions we take, until we discover that we had been that all along without being aware of it. The search does not stop there. We now become more observant of how we feel, and when and where we feel it. We learn to talk to our body. We become intimate with it. Our body is very precise and guides us to our next discovery, the next piece of the jigsaw we are doing.

Our emotions lead us to the next piece of the jigsaw. When we find it we handle it with care, we respect it and honour it, we bring it to our heart and love it. With each piece we find, we feel more ourselves, more whole. So the search continues.

The clues are everywhere around us. We just have to be in that vibration of wanting to clear our path. Our behaviour has a lot of clues, if we use our awareness. Working on our past lives, there are many to be found. Our interaction with others and the world at large is another source full of clues. Our reactions to our surroundings and thoughts, people and life also hold many clues. In short, clues are everywhere and in everything. We can become great detectives finding ourselves.

Have you experienced making a huge puzzle, with many small pieces, which took you a very long time to make? Then, you may remember that when you found a piece that fitted, you felt full of satisfaction or you may have felt exhilarated about it. Finding the pieces that fit in our lives is awesome. Are we looking for clues? Are we interested in finishing our puzzle in this lifetime, or do we want to carry on putting more layers to work in the next one? It is a concept that may not interest too many people. Pondering over it will not hurt anyone and it could benefit a lot of us tremendously. Those who are already enjoying this game can prove it. Yes, it is a game. The whole of our lives is a chain of games, which keep us hooked, making us believe that they are our reality. We fool ourselves thinking that it is so. Unfortunately, the price we pay is very high, higher than we dare to think, for if we stopped and thought, then the whole world would change. There would not be suffering, riots, wars, cruelty and crimes, all in the name of power.

If, before we go to sleep every day, we assess how our day went, what we did, how that affected the world around us and what we and others gained by our actions, it would be beneficial for everyone. If we were mindful and aware of our input in our lives and how that affected others and society at large, having criteria of wellbeing for ALL, the world would be a much better place to live in.

OPINIONS

· ·

We all have opinions. Stronger or weaker opinions come to us whether we like it or not because of human tendencies of thought and behaviour at any particular time in our lives. We are caught in that global wave of thought about whatever is happening at any particular time in history. Most people forget who they are and follow an illusionary path created by opinions. These can be theirs or someone else's and can become a strong rage, which goes beyond them. They get lost in these opinions without realising they are contaminating everyone else to a certain degree, regardless of whether they are agreeing with them or opposing them. This can be enough to create a conflict.

Those of us who do not want to be involved in other people's opinions have to be aware of what is going on and how that affects us, because if we follow the upheavals of others' opinions we lose our awareness and become as lost as them. Then, we cannot be of help to ourselves or anyone else either. We become entangled in the chaos and lose our stability and knowledge of who we really are. We allow the masses to pull us into their lack of consciousness and we may start echoing their words.

What should we do in these cases? Mainly, be calm. Be very calm. Bring our awareness to the forefront and realise we are not the opinions, which are short lived. We are much more. We go beyond the opinions and we live on. Our awareness will discern easily that we are not temporary opinions that come and go incessantly. However, if we wish to have opinions we can, provided we are aware that we are not those opinions and we can see the difference and separation between the two. For that to occur we must have a certain degree of inner knowledge, inner trust and be at one with the world and ourselves.

We have to remember that some people have an inflated ego and for that ego to be satisfied they need others to oppose it so as to create their battlefield. This can happen at many levels and through all aspects of life. We can see this in families, with friends, at work, socially and so on. It becomes a danger when it is in politics or religion, because it can take on exaggerated proportions, which can be difficult to control and can lead to great disasters for everyone and the planet in general. Our hope is that the work of all the carers of the planet, all those who are working for our wellbeing and the wellbeing of the collective, and the help we get from outside sources will be sufficient to counteract the madness of the few and the ignorance of the many.

Just imagine how wonderful the world would be if we were all compassionate and loving with the unconditional love that exists within us. Imagine if we could remember at all times that we are love and everyone else is too. Imagine if we could leave the past behind and be fully in our present moment, enjoying the fruits of the day. Imagine if we could dissolve all the programming we have inherited from our ancestors in addition to that forced on us by our parents and society. Imagine if we communicated more with nature and were as generous, as rich in abundance of what provides for us and as natural and humble in giving. Imagine if our hearts were more set on giving than on taking and rejoiced to see everyone happy. Imagine if we were to help those in need with a smile and a warm heart. Imagine if we were to encourage our young generation to be themselves rather than putting on them the burdens carried by other generations for so long. If these and many more ifs were put in place, we would be living in a world that everyone is looking for and wants to find. How much does it take from us to get there? Removing the "I", removing the "ego" and just being the natural beings we are would take us into consciousness of who we really are.

POWER

. . . .

On our planet the majority of humans are obsessed with power. Countless atrocities are committed in order to achieve power. It is usually power over others. By controlling others they can control their land and get the benefits the land offers. This obsession with power starts at a very early age, when they see in their family who is the person who controls and is the head of the family. In school they will see groups bullying other children. In their community there are also those who run things in their own way and no one dares to stand up to them. In groups of friends there is always one or a few who will decide what to do and where to go, regardless of the wishes of the other members of the group. This will follow on into higher education, university or no education at all. At work it is felt deeply, especially if the bosses are the kind of people who want those under them to know that they are in power from their abusive behaviour. When we get to religion and politics there is something else. Those two topics have been and still are the cause of much suffering on our beloved planet earth, and all because of Power.

By observing these phenomena of running after power, some of us do not quite understand the purpose of it and wonder if it is due to the projection programmed by them. If it is so, they have forgotten about it and go around living their projection as if it were their reality. So they do not know what they are doing because they have forgotten that these experiences in the physical world are temporary and our reality is infinite. However, nobody can tell these individuals that, because they will think we are out of our minds and will not pay attention to us.

On the other hand, we the observers can see that their search for power and the way they obtain it is horrendous and painful to everyone on the planet, including themselves. We could tell them, if they wanted to listen, that the power is within them already, that they could do wonderful things with it, they could create whatever they wished with it and fulfil themselves with their own creation for the benefit of all.

As for us, the observers, we carry on doing what we know best without judging anyone and bearing in mind that we are all part of the same energy, we are part of the Whole. This reality is there whether we believe it or not. All the projections taking place on earth are merely temporary for all of us, whether we like it or not. We are witnesses to a great display of games played sometimes very well and sometimes very badly. The players who think they are winners are usually the losers and the players just enjoying the game are the real winners. So, carry on playing and do not look at the score.

Fresh groups of players who know the games well are now coming to EARTH. They will make a difference to the games. They will change them for other more interesting ones and easier to play, where everyone will be able to participate and be allowed any role they may choose to play. That will make a beautiful playground where all players will know the rules of the game, and when it is their turn to play. Also, they will know when the game comes to an end for them and that will be accepted as naturally as carrying on playing. All players will be happy and all will be well. For those of us who will not be here long enough to see these games, let us enjoy the thought of those blissful days ahead for those who are coming to stay to play for that period of time. We will still be observing the new games from somewhere else and celebrating the joy of playing with them.

ACCEPTING

. . . .

When we have been waiting for a long time for something to happen two things can occur. We can get impatient and fiddly or accept the moment as it is. We can think we are wasting our time and that we could be doing something more useful. But there we are, not moving, just hoping that something will crop up, and we carry on with our day. It is quite a process to reach the core of our patience. It is a way to learn about ourselves and how we react in unexpected situations. It brings us a new perspective on how well or ill-prepared we are to deal with life as it comes, with unpleasant or pleasant surprises as they reach us.

When we become aware of the consecutive instances we are presented with and understand our behaviour, we have the chance to shift. We become very grateful and the awakening happens. It is like a ray of bright sun coming through a cloudy sky, surprising, amazing and dazzling us with its power of realising what is in front of us. We had not taken the time to look for it before. The consciousness and awareness is not a mystery. It is a fact. We are given so many opportunities to see and perceive what we do in our lives. But we do not seem to see them, because we only use our external vision.

Many of us have had the experience of being put in a situation we dislike tremendously, being angry at those who put us in it, directing our anger at them and then calming down. This can happen again and again until one day we decide to ask ourselves: Why are we so angry? Why do we have to get in that state? Why is that happening? How can it help us? After these questions the answers come in as clear as that bright ray of sunshine and hit us strongly. For a moment we cannot react. Our stillness makes the situation more powerful with the insight we are experiencing and we are in a completely different state of mind to our everyday one, far from the anger and impatience. Now there is a soothing feeling within us making us calm, kind, generous and understanding. We thank those who put us in that situation. Those individuals do not always know they are doing it, for there is an intelligent force that moves amongst us, guiding us to help each other. When we can see that, it feels we have achieved a great deal. It is all due to accepting the moment we are in and asking a few questions instead of running away with our negative thoughts and impatience. Having had one experience of this kind, we become alert to the possibility of other similar experiences and therefore are more sensitized to them.

The question we could ask ourselves is: why, in view of the above, are we still allowing so many instances to happen before we reach a solution? We have probably tried many ways of solving what we consider a problem. However, we fail over and over again, which leads us to extremes and blocks our flow of naturalness. Being blocked stops us from seeing the real picture, and we remain stuck, giving way to undesirable energies, which grow in size and in unpleasantness through repetition. Then, what do we do? Accepting the moment as it is without judgement, asking relevant questions without judgement, listening for the answers patiently without judgement, being kind and loving ourselves without judgement, these will be the ingredients necessary for us to come out of the blockage successfully. Once liberated from whatever issue, we are free to take action in the best way possible for everyone involved.

HAVE YOU NOTICED?

Have you noticed at times how, for no reason, we feel we hold something special in us, and as soon as that realisation comes the feeling goes away? A sensation of emptiness and longing is felt strongly and we are left in a wondering state. Other times, we are very awake when it happens and we know for sure that an important insight is coming. We welcome it with excitement, anticipation and joy in our heart. We reflect on the knowledge delivered and are grateful to be the recipient. How many times have you been in those situations? How many times have you ever noticed anything like that? You might have noticed it but did not attach any importance to it. After all, in your opinion it was not something you would go and tell people about. They may think you are out of your head talking nonsense. So many opportunities are lost in that way. So much knowledge is wasted, which adds to a field of blindness and lack of understanding amongst earthly people.

How would you solve the above? Whatever your suggestions, would you apply them to yourself and share those suggestions around you? Would you keep them to yourself and not think about them any more? If you do the latter, would you not be pinched, now and again, with a thought that would bother you? Living in a world where there are so many stimuli and wanting to do as many things as possible hardly leaves you time for any reflexion of this kind. Unless, of course, you are that way inclined.

At times, led by inertia or tiredness, you may find yourself watching a programme on the television which a member of the family has chosen and you sit and watch it with them. Through the film, you know you do not like it, you do not understand it but because you are so tired you do not move and carry on watching. Finally, at the end of the film, there is this strong feeling of discomfort and ill being, which you cannot account for. It may take you some time, if you are inquisitive and want to know the reason for it, but if you persist you will come to the conclusion that you have picked up the energies emanating from the characters in the film and their actions. For those who reach this point, how do you feel? Are you beating yourself up for having watched something you did not like anyway? Are you angry, still expressing the anger you picked up from the show? Are you blaming someone else for it? Whatever you do, make sure you take a decision to avoid doing something which is not to your liking. However, you know you have been in this kind of situation before and you are still doing it. What happens? Have you forgotten the last time it happened? What is driving you to make the same mistake again? Was it tiredness? Was it to please someone else? Was it because there was no other choice? Or were you simply not aware of your present moment? How many situations do you have in your life similar to this one? It may not be watching a show. It can be having a meal, discussing a project, going for a walk, taking a trip. Anything and everything can engage you in situations with disastrous aftermaths for yourself, your health and wellbeing.

Awareness of ourselves and our surroundings, respect and love for what we do, no matter how big or small, will keep us free from those situations. We will not only gain by having more time for ourselves but we will use it with joy and excitement in what we like doing most. We will find that when we do what we like doing, we not only enjoy life more but we do not get tired so easily and we have time for everything we wish to do.

Have you ever looked around at people and asked yourself, "How many of these faces show mindfulness?" Have you looked at yourself and asked the same question?

FORGETTING

By forgetting who they are, people create conflicts and suffering for themselves and for everyone else and they cry victory for their deeds. The frequent question "when are we going to learn?" does not refer to learning but to waking up from the illusion they take for reality. Since the majority of the population on the planet are living through that illusion, they take the lead in how the planet manifests their thoughts and actions by creating layers and layers of negativity, aggression and violence. That energy stays around influencing those who have similar tendencies or get close to that energetic wavelength.

Do you ever stop and ask yourself: What is going on here? What is happening? Am I cooperating in this? Who is this going to help? What is the purpose? How can it be measured? Asking questions opens up the field of options and solutions and stops the rush into violence and destruction.

Many people through the ages have been working to unite mind and body, which is fundamental for knowing who we are and therefore knowing also what our purpose in this present expression of ourselves on the planet is. There are great numbers of people at the moment following that movement, wanting to be whole, wanting to be one and not divided. This attitude contrasts with those whose ego drives them out of themselves and loses them in the illusion that separateness is the best and they can be in control. Their attention is totally on the outside world and that creates unbalance. They see the outside world as a possession they need to secure and control for fear that others will control them instead. They forget who they are, where they come from and what they came to do. They forget that they live in a most loved and beautiful planet that manifests our thoughts and wishes and gives us all we ask for without force, violence, selfishness or ego. This state of affairs disrupts and slows down the work that so many others are doing by remembering these very things.

We are mentioning the part of the population who are awakened and the other part who are not and strive to be very much on the opposite side. But there is another part that is in the middle. The ones who do not raise their voices to be heard are easily influenced by the flow of energies moving around them.

Imagine if we all woke up to our true reality and realised that what we thought was our reality is nothing but a dream, an illusion created by us, a project we decided to live through and enjoy on this planet. The obstacles were created to make us alert and make sure we do not forget who we are, so we can succeed in our adventure. Imagine we have all the power anyone can desire and more but we just have to remember who we are so we can tap into it. Imagine there is no separation but the one we create ourselves in our illusion of the role we want to play. Imagine that we remember at all times that whatever role we play, it is just a game which we can stop any time we wish, start again or change. Imagine we are like children in a set of games and roles we can choose from and enjoy. Imagine that, even though we are all very different, we are all made of the same dough and belong to the same creator, who is vigilant of our behaviour and cares for our wellbeing at all times. Imagine that those people who we may think are our enemies are there only to help us grow and find a skill in us that we designed ourselves when we created the project we are living through. Imagine, that all of it is our reality.

PEACE, LOVE, FREEDOM

. . . .

In the silence of our soul we find the peace, love and freedom that everyone is looking for, and yet not many are looking in that special place for those things. Do you know why? Has it occurred to you to look in there? How many times have you looked? Or have you never done it or even thought of doing it? These questions come up because the masses want to get all this from outside themselves and expect to be given it by others who may be in the same situation. So it is like turning around in circles and never finding the way out. Although they may never stop on their way, they cannot get out of the track in which they are turning in circles with the same ideas in mind. It is a curious fact that we can be looking for something and, even though it is in front of us, we may not see it at all. It is as if the limits of our vision stop us from seeing.

PEACE, LOVE, FREEDOM: magical words. We could wonder whether their definition is clear and understood by those who fight so fiercely to find the state of being the words seem to offer. If we were to look back in history, we would find the most tragic chain of wars and upheavals at a global level and all of them for the sake of defending those words. Have we moved forward? Clearly and sadly no, we have not. We have not because there are still upheavals and wars currently using those words as shields to hide their greed, ego, and whatever else.

There are minorities screaming loudly to everyone who wants to listen that the world is supposed to be governed in a different way. These minorities offer teachings and insights into how to go about obtaining what others say they are fighting for.

Those who coach will frequently find clients who are afraid of looking inside themselves. A fear comes over them, paralysing the session, just because they cannot look inside themselves. It is a fear they cannot explain or understand. As the coach approaches the issue in other ways, it transpires that the clients are afraid of themselves and of what they may find by looking inside, in the depths of themselves.

How often do we think of the consequences of our thoughts and actions that will follow those thoughts? How often do we think that if our house is not cleaned and in order, we cannot ask our neighbours to have theirs cleaned and in order? How often do we check when something happens in our lives, that is not pleasant or brings suffering, to see if our thoughts on the subject had something to do with it? Everyone is free to think, but nobody wants to take on the outcome of their own thoughts. It is easier to blame others for it. Have you noticed that as soon as something unpleasant or that grieves you happens in your life, you find some reason or somebody to blame? It is as if you consider that it is not your fault and has nothing to do with you. However, our true selves do not work like this. If you want to be honest and true to yourself, you may have to find out what is inside you. If you are afraid to look inside by yourself, then there are many professionals such as coaches, healers and others who will be able to help you to start the journey of discovering who you really are and how much is activated by the way you think and not what others do to you. Ignoring this fact can only perpetuate misunderstandings and keep you away from enjoying life to its fullest. Observing our thoughts will give us the answers to how we live and what is in our lives. We may be very surprised not only by what we may find but also by the fact that we have had it there all the time and we were not aware of it. So, now that we are, we can make important changes to our lives and ourselves.

GETTING UP IN THE MORNING

Getting up in the morning when most people are still sleeping; looking through the window to feel as if the trees are still sleeping too; breathing the stillness of the moment and just being in it for a while, soaking in it; being aware of the importance of our breath and feeling it, in and out of our body, with sensations of connecting with the whole universe; being aware and grateful for all of this is a wonderful potion with which to start the day, for it sets us in a brand new starting point and we can look ahead to a successful day.

How many of us are doing this? Just imagine the benefits that would accrue in our personal life. Just imagine going to work with a smile on our face, being grateful for the new day, the job and the colleagues we work with. Just imagine that we leave behind everything that does not serve us or anyone else any longer, making us lighter as we leave behind useless weight. Just imagine being one hundred per cent in everything we do. Our contentment would be contagious and we would put everyone in a good mood, with the possibility that others would follow suit and become equally content. Can we see how easy it would be to create a loving world to live in? It has been said that in our sleep we clear everything from the day before. Therefore we are given a chance to change things for the better. Starting the day with a fresh and new outlook would put us in the right frame of mind to pursue our goals in life.

How we spend our day depends entirely on us. If we allow the interactions, situations, meetings with people, deals that fall through and other issues to push us out of our centre, then we get lost in the madness of society. However, if we keep our serenity, contentment and sense of wellbeing, we will be unshakable and nothing will take us out of our centre. Of course, where there are doubts there are weaknesses. Where there are weaknesses there will be giving in to whatever comes our way and that is how we can get lost. Being aware is the clue, because if we are aware we take everyone and everything into consideration including ourselves. That will give us room to consider and reconsider the path we want to take. We may wish to be in the entanglement of life or we may wish to be out of it. The choice is always ours, whether we believe it or not, whether we accept it or not. We are the ones who decide at every moment what to do with our life. Sometimes, the human collective drives us into situations that we cannot avoid. It is usually political, religious or any other thing people go into without questioning themselves about where they are going.

Having gone through what a day can give and how we can manage it, the rest is left to us. We can do or undo whatever suits our needs and our wellbeing, according to the kind of life we chose to be in when we came to the planet. Once we are here, it is a bit late to complain. We chose those experiences. We keep choosing our daily experiences. We may feel like protesting and denying that fact, but then we are denying ourselves and until we are very clear in our understanding of being where we are, we would always have an inner conflict. So the best way is to find out. Learn and do what we came to do without a fuss. Everyone will be happier for it. Especially ourselves. Life is beautiful if we let it be. The Universal Intelligence is working alongside us, guiding us provided we allow it. Are we going to resist it or allow it? Does it need thinking about? If it does, hurry up!

PLANET EARTH

. . . .

These days there are so many natural ways of healing that we can choose from. Sometimes, the choice is difficult unless we know what we want. We could also feel attracted to what is good for us by our own body. Those remedies have always existed, but through the changes in political power a lot of them were lost or went underground and were practised by the very few. Now, it is a pleasure to see so many healing practices and such a great number of practitioners. The list is too long to be written here. One of the good things of living in the digital world is that we can find what we want really fast on the internet and finding a healer of our choice is at our fingertips in seconds.

It is not our intention here to go into the different types of healing. Knowing that they exist is sufficient. We would like to bring attention to Nature, Mother Earth, Gaia, whatever name we use for her. There are many earth carers doing a lot of work for her, but it is a minority if we take into account the millions existing and living on her. Do we think about our beautiful planet as the one that keeps us alive? Have the impressive sites of nature touched us? By its beauty and diversity? By its fauna? Do we teach our children where everything comes from: that our physical bodies, our houses and belongings, our ways of travelling and everything manmade belong to the earth? The most important things are food for our sustenance, herbs to heal us and beauty to rejoice in. The variety of healing herbs is enormous. Herbalists are still finding new ones.

There is so much to say about the earth. Those of us who love our planet and feel our heart in hers are very grateful and thankful. She is our best teacher. If we take the time to observe natural life around us, we would be amazed at what we can discover. We can see her power when we spot a lovely flower coming out from a crack in dry, bare land where there has not been a drop of water for ages and, looking around, nothing else seems to be alive in the vegetable world but this amazing flower. If faced with that fact, would we not stop and think of that immense power and ponder that we are part of that power too? Mother Earth, as a mother would, is showing us and proving to us that everything is possible, if we put our mind to it and believe it.

When things do not go the way we would want them to and the mind is in turmoil, by sitting next to a tree or looking at it from a short distance, allowing the tree to talk to us, Mother Earth surprises us by making that tree change shapes so that we understand what is going on within us. It will give us the shape, which will guide us to know what path to take. This is an amazing fact.

As for healing plants, real herbalists, who love healing plants, know how to listen to them, and they also know by instinct what a particular plant is able to do. It is all part of the caring love the earth has for us all. If only we took some time to observe what the earth does, how she does it, to whom she does it and for what purpose. Then, we would understand so many things that would bring us to realise what we are doing. It would make us realise also that we are our own enemies and that we already have all we need to be happy and enjoy life on earth as a paradise, rather than struggling through it thinking how hard it is to live. All it needs is to be aware of who we are and our purpose for being here. From those of us who are aware and care, THANK YOU.

DYING

Dying is a word that scares us in the same way the unknown scares us. Not knowing what is going to happen and ending that which is known are things we do not want to think about, until they affect us in loved ones or in people close to us. Then we have to accept them. Many find it difficult to go through this experience of losing someone important in their lives. But that is because they lack the wisdom of knowing why we are here, why we have come and what will happen when we leave. Even with this knowledge it can be hard for us to detach ourselves from the terrestrial world that many of us believe is our reality.

We are not what we think we are. This is not our reality. It is a manifested dream that has an end, but we do not finish when the dream does. We are a projection of the dream. In the same way, here on earth we plan projects regarding what we are going to be, our family, if we are going to have children, where we are going to live, the trips we are going to take, and so on. That is what we have done before arriving on our beloved planet earth. We have planned everything we wanted to do and the experiences we wanted out of our project. In this project, as in those we may have here on earth, we are given the freedom to change ideas and to change the project according to what we find along the way. This project has a time limit, as do those we undertake on earth. When the planned time comes to an end, we have to leave, whether we have finished the project or not. What has been happening is that after the first years arriving on earth, we forget everything we are, where we have come from, and how to get our project started and functioning. If we had not forgotten, we would have wanted to go back when we encountered our first difficulties. Now though, for a long time, many beings have been arriving who do not forget who they are. They come already knowing what they are going to find, but with the difference that they do not forget who they are and where they come from, so they are prepared to face these challenges.

We are infinite beings. We have always existed and we will always exist. We only have our physical body in order to exist on earth. It is the same as having a car to go from one place to another. When a car is of no use to us, we change it for another. Cars are simply a means of transport. That is all. It is the same with our physical body. Almost all our earthly trajectory has been planned before coming to live it. Changes happen according to the freedom we have and as we remember who we are and where we come from.

If we consciously revised our lives, we would be surprised at what we would find. If we stayed in internal silence during a period of meditation in order to reach our deeply hidden inner Self, we would be able to see the light we are made of. It would be like awakening to a new unknown world, even though it is our world, so real and well known to us. Sometimes projects infect us in such a way that we come to believe we are the very project we are working on, thus easily forgetting our identity. If we come to this realisation, what remains for us to do is to find the path that leads us to the connection by which we identify with our true Self.

WHEN YOUR HEART CALLS YOU

When your heart calls you, listen to it. It has important information to give you that only it can give you. Follow the instructions it gives you, for if you don't you will regret it.

How often do we disregard calls from our heart? Innumerable times. We brush those calls aside as if they have not been heard and carry on with whatever mundane things we are doing.

There are times when we feel the urge for adventure and have magnificent ideas; we play with those ideas in our mind. We get excited. We enjoy them. Then when we get to the point of doing what is in our mind, we stop and give up. Why do we give up? What is it that can stop those great ideas? Many things can crop up on our list where we don't follow our heart. It would be a sad day if we followed those excuses on the list and abandoned the call from the heart. For the heart is fresh and alive, full of enthusiasm and motivation, ready to jump. The heart does not know fear because in it dwells the eternal being that is us. If we follow the list of excuses, we are following our intellect, which only deals with the temporal and becomes frightened easily since it lacks a vision of the future. On the list are also the many aspects of the ego, hidden in what appear to be good reasons not to pursue our dreams.

Listening to our heart when we meet what seems to be a new person would be beneficial for both parties. Listening to our heart carefully, we hear that the new person is not new; we know each other from other time lines and our meeting is not a coincidence. It has been programmed so that we finish what we were doing in that other existence; or maybe, we had planned to meet up on this planet to enjoy what we had planned together. Here is when we are going to be very still and calm and allow our heart to guide us in what would be best for everyone.

Our behaviour when meeting people we had previously encountered in a past life can shock us. These meetings can occur in different fields of life. The following is a real example, which illustrates it:

There is a course we want to do and we have to go before a panel to be interviewed. We are well prepared and we know it. As soon as we look into the eyes of the members of the panel, we identify one member who keeps his eyes on ours as if wanting to defeat us. We can be shocked for it is the first time we have set eyes on that person. How can he look at us with such hate? In ourselves, we know this member of the panel is going to reject our being accepted for the course we so much want to go on. He does. We are denied this opportunity. We are so disappointed that we go out of our way to investigate why this situation has had such an outcome. The answer is that we were enemies in another life, at war, and we killed this person. When we know this, the disappointment dissolves as we can see how the energies are levelling and instead of feeling resentment towards that person, we quickly see a new avenue for us to focus on, leaving behind the incident of the interview.

This can happen in any situation in life. It can go even further. We can be listening to a member of our family or a friend talking about a new member of staff they have in their office, and as we hear what is being said we feel discomfort in our body. We feel strange and a dislike for that person creeps up from nowhere, because we have never met the person. By following our heart we will find the answer.

On the other hand, we can find the opposite situation when we meet someone for the first time. There can be a warm feeling as if we had known him or her all our lives and there is a connection from heart to heart. Our heart is talking to us using unconditional love. Our ego or our earthly programming by parents and society can spoil this precious pure love, because we ignore the advice from the heart. When your heart calls you, listen very carefully and follow it, for it will take you where your dreams exist and there will be no regrets.

WORRYING ABOUT OTHERS

orrying about others is something we do well. We worry about our family members, friends, neighbours, colleagues and the world at large. Why do we worry? Is worrying helping anyone? By putting our attention on what worries us, we are increasing the problem we are worrying about, so we are not helping. Help will come when we bring our attention to where we want to see others and ourselves enjoying life and being happy, because that will give the help needed to improve the situation we have in mind.

By going deep into ourselves, we will find that the worry we may have is one of the essences of fear. Worrying is fear. Dissolving fear is an effective way of dealing with the situation. It will also lead us to where we are supposed to be in relation to the object of our worry. We know we want to help whenever possible and it will be useful to remember that if we allow our inner guidance to lead us into what we are supposed to do, we will be successful.

If we go deep, deep down into ourselves, we will see that the worry is not about anyone but ourselves. Keeping our understanding at that level of depth, we can see how interconnected we are. In fact, we are worrying about ourselves through someone else.

By being centred, we will know when to act and when to step aside and let life take its course, remembering at all times that what we see and understand is not what others see and understand. Therefore, our interference without approval or request from those we want to help would be an intrusion. Frequently, with our eagerness to help, we may want to convince them that we have solutions at hand that will help them. However, let us remember that our solutions are not necessarily other people's solutions, for we have different paths to walk and different experiences to encounter and deal with. Nevertheless, we want to remain available for any opportunity that comes our way in which we can be of help.

By leaving behind worrying, we will be in a better place to find the abundance any situation requires, so that all will be well. We are only witnesses of what goes on around us. Our intention is that all there is to witness is the wellbeing of everyone, with the knowledge that we are all where we are supposed to be at every moment of our lives.

WHEN WE ARE BORN

B efore we are born, we have prepared our arrival well on the planet and we have chosen our parents according to the experiences they can offer us and we want to experience on earth. When we are in the non-physical state before coming, any difficulties we may see do not stop us because everything is easy from that perspective and we are free from the burdens that the physical world will put on us. It is when we are ready to arrive on earth that some of us will feel pulled back. Suddenly, in front of us, are the pictures of what our life will be like and we may want to change our mind about coming. We know one such case well.

A spirit who was ready to incarnate and become an earthly child had second thoughts about it and wanted to go back, just at the moment of arrival. This being was told that it was too late and it had to continue the journey chosen with its specific programme attached to it. The child refused and made efforts to go back, but instead found it had been pushed down and the impact of that push was a very sudden birth, to the surprise of the new mother and those around her. More surprised was the baby to find itself in a physical body, which it could not manage and surrounded by people who did not know what to do with the newborn. This happened when the mother was happily talking to her own mother and a friend in the kitchen and she felt this rush of the baby within her coming out. She ran to the bedroom and her experience of giving birth lasted minutes despite it being her firstborn.

We wonder how many babies change their mind about coming to visit us before they are born. If you are reading this, are you one of them? Do you remember your arrival and the reasons why you wanted to go back and cancel the process you were in?

For those of us who suffered this kind of predicament, we have to wait to go back to know the details and reasons for that strong wish not to go on with our projection at that particular time. Some of you may already know. There is a book called "Memories from Heaven" by Dr. Wayne Dyer, where one can find a collection of memories from children before they were born, from around the world. Unlike the children in the book, we have lost our memories of where we came from and what it was like, why we wanted to come and what our project was in coming. A lot of terrestrial humans do not remember those facts and do not even believe in their possibility. We would say to those people to look inside, without judgement, and observe how they feel by asking themselves some questions.

The earth is changing so rapidly. Time seems to have shrunk. One hears frequently the fact that there is no time or that time goes so fast, the weeks pass very quickly and so do the years. So most people have the feeling of acceleration in time and now there are those who are starting to ask questions about it. It is an exciting time we are awakening into, to get to know who we really are and where we come from. Through these big changes, it is sad that there is also tremendous pain and disasters to encompass the changes. It is important to bring the awakening into our lives as soon as possible to put ourselves in a position where, through our understanding of the process, we can be more prepared for it and can help those in need of a hand to make the journey.

Let us all remember that we came from the light and we will go back to the light. We are infinite beings who are expanding through the universe. Let us enjoy this time on earth and be grateful for the opportunity of being here now.

I AM SO GRATEFUL

• •

Being grateful, for some of us, is a powerful feeling within us, which bursts out in silence for we are at a loss as to how to express it. It is too big and complex for us to find ways with words, which would be identical to our feelings. We are so lucky to wake up in the morning into a new day in which we are given the opportunity of renewal, of changes, of expansion, of looking ahead with a new perspective and so many paths to choose from. If only we were aware. From being aware comes the great feeling of gratefulness.

When we are in that space of awareness we can see our day by day development progressing with the events we bring to it. There is a special touch in what we do, improving and smoothing our actions and, on occasions, bringing us relief. It is especially noticeable when we are facing a situation that we consider difficult to deal with. It is then we are surprised at what happens to us. We are in awe because we are aware of how the situation changes in front of our eyes to make it easier for us. We cannot help thinking that it was done especially for us. There could be millions of people affected in the same way, but we feel it personally as if it was just done for us because we had asked for it and it was delivered, even better than what we asked for. We are tempted to call those instances 'miracles' because they impress us so.

When we are grateful, the energy of that feeling surrounds us and can be seen by others. There is no need for words. It is a touching energy, which connects the person who is grateful to the source of his or her gratefulness. This feeling is also a kind of miracle because of its power and the impact that it has on us.

There are so many things to be grateful for that it would be impossible to name them all. Who cannot be grateful for the complexity and intelligence of each cell in our body and the amazing work those cells are constantly doing for the duration of our life? Who could not be grateful for our health, family, friends and everyone and everything around us that makes a difference to our wellbeing and happiness? Who can be indifferent to the beauty of nature, presented to us in so many ways? For example, we say 'breathtaking' when admiring a view we have no words to describe how we feel. Would we not be grateful for enjoying that experience? How about our breath? We wonder at how many people on waking up in the morning think of their breath and are grateful for it. Thinking of our breath and being grateful for it is an important way of starting our day.

When some people are grateful, it tends to be for things that go well in their lives and not for those things that give them pain. However, the latter ones can be blessings in disguise. In time, those unpleasant events will reveal a favourable situation matching just what they had wanted. Being grateful brings abundance in our life and our life is full of reasons to be grateful. We are grateful to Mother Earth and its whole creation and to the seasons that challenge our senses, to the water that makes rivers and oceans, to the air we breathe, to the sun, the moon and the whole Universe. We are grateful when we look at a flower and we melt in its beauty. We are grateful if we are able to climb the high peaks of mountains and feel the overwhelming elation in that altitude. We are grateful to the Universal Intelligence within us, guiding and helping us incessantly. We do not think there is anything at all we cannot be grateful for. WE ARE GRATEFUL.

A SMILE

Agenuine, kind, warm and loving smile on a face is a powerful tool. It can melt the hardest of hearts. Have you noticed that? Become aware of the right smile for there are many kinds.

A smile is like an invitation from the heart to be who you are. A smile accepts you unconditionally. It creates a warm feeling that allows and welcomes you. It is easy to communicate with others through that kind of smile.

A smile opens the door to the heart and makes understanding simple, fast and to the point without a need for superfluous explanations.

A warm smile is comforting to all of us at any time and in any place. We just love it.

Our nature prompts us to smile at all times. As a baby or small child the prompting pulls us, and as we grow up we override the prompting and replace it with influences from outside. There are some who may be saved and continue to be natural.

Being natural means we follow our inner guidance and flow effortlessly through our path of life without being overcome by turbulences we may encounter on the way. Our smile reassures us that all is well.

A smile on a face is beautiful and invites us to join in. Have you noticed? When someone greets us with a smile, we respond by smiling back. There are so many instances where a smile has changed or saved a situation, opened a dialogue between strangers and served as a sign of agreement in difficult cases. We all have many more situations to account for.

A smile on a face radiates warmth and light, changing the atmosphere around it – just like the sun in the sky radiates light and warmth to the earth.

We are all bearers of that kind of smile. It is worth checking to make sure we are using it. Denying this gift is like denying life itself. Could we live without the sun? To a lesser degree, a smile affects us in the same way.

A smile has been the inspiration for poets. They were and are able to see the qualities and beauty of it and they could and can transfer them into poems or poetical prose.

Can you imagine anyone with a warm and loving smile being angry? Depressed? Frustrated? No, because that kind of smile is calming and inviting to our natural wellbeing.

If your smile is not frequently with you, check it out. Where could it be lost? Find it and bring it back to shine on your face so that you can make others remember their own smile too and prompt them to look for it, in case they have lost it too.

AUTUMN

Autumn is a season of the year that reminds us of the temporary nature of our stay on earth. The trip is short like many others that we have already experienced but do not remember. There are also people who do not believe we have been on earth before, in other bodies and lives totally different from now. However, knowledge on this subject is spreading rapidly.

Autumn also reminds us of that end, of that finish without ties, of that letting go without looking back, without holding on to what we believed was a reality when it was really only a dream. It makes us look beyond ourselves and embrace our true reality. It makes us strong and happy looking forward to our arrival, because the trip has been tiring and we want to rest.

Autumn is cheerful with bright reds, yellows, oranges and greens. It is a feast of natural colours that is offered to us as a gift of nature and another lesson to learn. Living it with joy is a delight for the soul, and learning the lesson is our preparation for continuing through this life.

Autumn is the season that invites us to prepare for rest and contemplation, to review our adventures around the planet and perhaps repair some, to look forward without thinking we are leaving something behind, to feel strong and to be able to say that everything is fine and we are where we should be.

Autumn dresses up to impress us and tell us that the best is yet to come.

Autumn, if we listen to it, has much to say. Let's stop hurrying and see where it wants to take us. We feel its warm whisper, its advice that guides us on the path we have to follow. Make no mistake: what seems like an end is just another beginning.

Autumn invites us to stop on the way and examine what we are doing, so that we will not have to think, "I wish I had known that".

What else does autumn tell us? There is so much more that it would be impossible to write it all down. However, those of us who listen already know it, and if we do not we want to find out. As a result, we find it on our way as if magically presented to us.

Let us celebrate autumn with all its colour and all its teachings. Let us share what we know, and thus help those we can. Let us open our hearts to real life and know what we are, where we come from, and where we will go. Let us be confident and always think everything is fine. We are the ones who have the reins of our lives in our hands and can change our lives whenever we want. Some may say that this is not possible, but we will have to remind them that wherever they are they have arrived there on their own two feet. We are the ones who co-create our lives. We may know that, or we may ignore it. That is the reality. Let us not be blinded by excuses.

May there be many autumns in our lives and may we know how to celebrate them with joy.

BEING AT ONE

· ·

What do we understand by being at one? We hear so many people saying they are at one. We are all one. We all belong to each other. Most of the times when I hear the sound of these words I can also hear the vacuum from within the words. They lack the meaning from within. They sound hollow and empty. In the majority of cases there is no essence in them or in the experience they offer.

Words can be heard and repeated parrot-like. Words become fashionable and people use them without criteria. If we move into circles of personal development, spiritual growth or such like, we will hear the genuine sounds in their full meaning; but the majority of people present will be just repeating what they hear others say or what some leaders, gurus, teachers ask them to say.

We find that in religions as well. A majority of people gather in their particular sacred places to pray together and to follow the sacred words from those Gods they believe in; and yet, as soon as the prayers are over many go back to their habits. The sacred words have only touched their lips. The meaning and depth of the words evades them, in spite of the hard work some put into spreading the knowledge and helping others to understand it.

There are also those people who experience the knowledge and feel it in their own lives, so when they speak, their words reach the hearts of those who listen to them, because their words are charged with universal power that only carries love, compassion and wellbeing for all. These people do not have to say much, but what they say means more than hours of speeches telling others what to do.

Native Americans ask: "do you walk your talk?" They go more by what the heart says in silence than what the mouth says in sounds. When we can communicate from heart to heart, we are communicating in depth. We can say WE ARE AT ONE because our hearts are engaged in the same feeling and it is easy for us to merge, energetically speaking, with anyone and everyone.

Listening to our hearts and paying attention to what we hear will take us where we want to be and will help us to find all the requirements needed to achieve our goals in life, in harmony with other terrestrial beings who are on their journey as well. Sometimes we may be inclined to join in with others who will teach us what we want to know. Other times, we will be teaching them what they want to know. There is no need to say we are teachers or students, because our hearts have put us in a situation of equals, where the concept will not even come up, for we are always teachers and students at the same time.

BEING AT ONE. We like feeling at one because we can dissolve into everything, everyone and everywhere. When we are in that state of oneness we are feeling our true selves. We know that is what we are. It is an empowering feeling that fills us with confidence and wellbeing. We also know if it is true or false when individuals tell us that they are at one, because we can sense it in our hearts. It is as if a red or green light comes on informing us of what has been said. If our sensation equals the red light, we do not judge what has been said. We surround the individuals with compassion and love knowing that the oneness exists in them already. If our sensation equals the green light we will feel it strongly as being at one.

REJECTION

I f in our journeys through life we have experienced rejections that hurt and impacted on us, that alone will create a sensitivity in us which will make us react in certain subtle cases where no rejection is intended. These situations can create regrettable misunderstandings, which could lead to a dead end instead of to fruitful outcomes.

A rejection can take many forms and there is an equal number of ways in which it can be received. We enjoy great diversity of people on the planet, all of whom have different cultures and therefore see rejection differently.

If we have been rejected once and that was painful and nothing was done to remove the pain, then the pain is still with us and will cause us harm. Mainly, because we will be attracting more of the same through fear, we will be so sensitive to any word or gesture that even the intonation of a sentence will immediately make our emotional body react by withdrawing from the situation or the people involved. These incidents will add layers and layers of the same on us. That can make us react very quickly and withdraw from people, jobs, friendships and relationships. It may even affect us with family members, who we know well. We can lose many opportunities and friendships. Nobody told us how to deal with it. No one helped us. We did not know. What can we do?

It is important to be aware of how we feel, ask questions as to why we are feeling that way, examine the answers that may come up and observe where we stand. Do we feel strong or vulnerable? If we feel strong, we will know how to proceed. If we feel vulnerable, we start by finding out what reasons make us vulnerable or by getting help. We consider very intelligent those who will ask for help and accept it, instead of staying stuck. As human beings we all need each other, whether we like it or not. We all have something valuable to share and help others with. In the same way, the tools of others can help us.

Rejections from parents, teachers, friends, partners, or anyone in the street can all cause an impact, depending on how we are. So many situations can be solved if only we stop and assess them. If we do not know how, ask for help. These days help is everywhere to choose from in a variety of approaches.

There are people we want to know better and make friends with. We reach out and they say something. Maybe they hesitate in a sentence or are surprised in a questionable way at what we say. That will be enough for us to withdraw, feeling a deep thread of pain from far beyond our understanding. Our self-esteem gets a knock down and that makes the pain stronger. All this is happening on our side, because on the side of those other people we wanted to interact with there is no intention of rejection at all. In fact, in many cases the opposite is true. However, having been hurt badly once by rejection, any small thing can trigger in us the same pain and maybe we bring into the present the scenario of many time lines before this one. We would like to suggest paying attention to the present moment and how we feel at all times; so as not to miss out on having great friends and opportunities of success in our present journey.

What seems to be is not really what it is, even though we insist on making it be, according to our perception of the moment.

WE WISH

. . . .

We wish that those who are sleeping would wake up. We wish that those who are on their way to wakening would keep working on themselves to be in their centres and would not allow themselves to be influenced by those who are going in the opposite direction. We wish that the awakened keep working, as they already do, to bring light into the darkness, so that everyone can see and there will not be anywhere to hide the illusion of what the sleeping ones think is their reality.

It is painful to see nations fighting with each other, but it is still more painful to see a nation fighting within itself. The pain goes deeper when those who we thought were into knowledge and the reality of life suddenly follow the influence of others and become vulnerable and swayed by their illusory ideas. We would like to remind them, if we may, of all the hours they have spent learning and following courses, going to seminars and workshops internationally (some of them), and also of the many people they engaged with talking about what we are doing on this planet and how to make everyone understand that by hurting someone else we are hurting ourselves. We would do well to remember that every thought we send out will come back to us manifesting just what we sent out. It is not a question of believing it or not, it is a universal law that no one can stop or escape from.

We suggest moments of silence within ourselves. Restful moments of the mind, where there are no thoughts, no noise, just silence. These moments are precious because they put us in our vortex, in our centre; we get back our balance and see the way out of any situation bringing the best solution for everyone.

The idea of power, which people are running after, is futile. In a few seconds anything can be destroyed. Whole countries can be ruined. There is no manpower that can prevent it. The important thing to remember is that life is what we make of it as individuals and masses. We will have to deal at our personal level with what we put out. We will harvest the seeds we plant. The same goes for the masses. Whatever the masses put out, that is what they will get back. Blaming others is not taking responsibility for our thoughts and actions. There is never anyone to blame but ourselves, and yet we are not to be blamed either, because if we behave in ways that have important repercussions on the world and ourselves, it is due to our being asleep. The call to wake up is at our door.

Attachment has a lot to do with being aloof to our reality. People get so attached to their belongings and everything they think they possess that they forget who they are. They give themselves identities and can go to war to defend them. They consider themselves above others. And that, they think, gives them the right to dictate to others and do as they please.

Fear is what people use in order to subdue the masses. Any kind of fear will do. So many fall for that trick. It is sad to see so much suffering through fears. However, fear is the ingredient used by so many to control countries. It is done in many ways, which look genuine enough to those who fall in the trap and suffer the consequences of it. Being in fear is being a slave to those who instigate it.

We advocate freedom. The place to find it is in our inner silence. Be awake. Be your real YOU.

THE BARRIERS OF MISUNDERSTANDING

Sometimes we find ourselves engaged in conversations with others thinking we are talking about the same thing, until we realise the flow is stopped as if by a barrier which denies communication. It is an incredible sensation feeling the ground under our feet moving and we want to hold on to something to secure our topic in a way we understand it. However, others have a different understanding and, no matter how many explanations and proofs we present to them, they are not going to change their opinion. That leaves us somehow depleted. We have wasted energy without the joy of being understood. We do not have to agree with each other all the time for us to enjoy our discussions.

What can we do in these cases? Before we start talking choose the subject that goes with the person we are talking to. Observation would be beneficial in these situations. We could also talk about general things and allow the flow of conversation to take its course. Asking questions is always a winner, because everyone wants to talk about themselves or give opinions about the world and its affairs. The trick here is to be mindful, and not tread in sensitive areas that could bring us to the blockages we have already mentioned.

There are also other barriers that could be a mystery to us. We meet people with whom we get on splendidly well. There is a special connection between the other person and us. The feeling is quite extraordinary. We could have met this person a few days ago and yet we feel as if we had known them all our lives. When we talk we sense a warmth and understanding from the heart in a childlike innocence and beauty. We become aware of this and love the moments spent with this person. It makes us feel close at a different level of existence. We do not talk about it. We go with the feeling and allow it to speak in silence, expressing what words could not express. It is exempt from physical desires, for what we feel is above all that. It is felt on both sides and yet no one speaks about it. However, one day it can happen that the beautiful encounter breaks up with the impact of a precious and loved glass object falling on the floor and breaking into pieces. We are dismayed for we cannot find a reason for it. We suddenly sense a cold feeling where there was a warm one. All the good sensations have ceased, leaving in us a great vacuum with lots of unanswered questions.

What can we do in these cases? Watch out for the resentment we could feel towards that person. We do not know their reasons for the sudden change and behaviour. We keep calm. Being in our centre we will be alright. Accepting and being grateful for such an experience makes us more understanding, helping us to be detached, free and richer for the experience.

Silencing our mind for periods of time will lead us to what the right thing to do is and when. Often, questions asked at the wrong time receive the wrong answers. Had they been asked at the right time, they would have had satisfactory ones.

It is up to us to see possible barriers of misunderstanding and dissolve them before they become a problem in our lives. One thing we will never do is blame others for what happens to us. Blaming others is a sign of weakness and lack of responsibility. Understanding works on both sides. However, if we feel the other side to be tight we can allow the flow, even though we keep out of it. That way we will avoid the unpleasantness of communication and misunderstanding.

TIREDNESS

When we are tired we become different people, even to ourselves. Our patience disappears. We are irritable and anything can trigger a change of mood into something we do not feel at ease with. Our energy decreases and we are slow in our body and mind. Our reflexes also are affected, because we do not react at the speed the situations we are in require. We may say and do the wrong thing, which we will regret later or straight away. All this takes place just because we are tired and we do nothing about it.

Sometimes this occurs without us realising we are tired. Other times, we know we are tired but will not do anything about it and carry on with the activities we are doing, ignoring completely our state of being. It can happen that we are so much into what we are doing that we are not aware of it. For instance: when we are working on a project, when we are carried away by duties, when we rush from one thing to the other without any rest, when we do not eat well or regularly, when we do not give the body the rest it needs and abuse it in different ways, when we are playing games. We could carry on with the list.

Have we considered the damage that being tired can do to us at all levels? Have we done anything about it?

Managing our lives can help tremendously. There will always be extreme situations when we are forced to put up with whatever comes to us, at least for a while. However, changes are a way of getting out of those situations that create tiredness. Sometimes a small change can turn a life upside down in any direction we desire. A clear and rested mind would help the changes considerably. For the mind to be rested, it needs silence, inner silence. We can be anywhere, doing anything, surrounded with lots of noise and people and we can still persuade our mind to be silent. In this state of being, we know what is best for us and also how we can achieve it. We become intuitive as to which path to take and how to direct our lives by enjoying good health and getting the most out of what is around us.

Being aware of how the body feels will give us the signs we need to know how to proceed in making changes in our lives. If we practise being in the silence of the mind, awareness follows and knowledge as what to do is present too. Our sensitivity increases and the signs will be so obvious to us that they cannot be ignored. That will give us the opportunity to make any changes we consider necessary in order to keep tiredness away.

We accept tiredness in our lives as if it were a necessity and keep talking about it, reinforcing it and giving it space to grow even bigger, instead of eliminating it and throwing it out of our state of being. Managing our lives, being aware, silencing the mind regularly, refusing to accept tiredness as a part of us, being engaged with things that we are interested in and enthuse us, having the courage to say no and enjoying saying yes when the situation requires it are all part of keeping tiredness away.

Let us remember, once more, the magnificent beings we are. Let us remember we can change and do anything we wish to.

JUDGEMENT

. . . .

"Don't judge if you don't want to be judged." This saying is a good reminder.

Sometimes we judge without realising we are judging. Other times we judge with full awareness. People have a tendency to judge others and what they do. It is interesting how we put ourselves in a position where we believe that what we think is always THE WAY and any other way is the wrong way. This position does not help anyone and removing it benefits everyone.

By judging others we are judging ourselves. This realisation is sufficient to stop us from doing it. However, there are those who are very hard on themselves, criticising their gifts and how they use them. Those with depressive tendencies know this well. They are hard and negative in judging what they are and what they do.

If we look around we can see that we live in a judgemental society. The media is full of it. In fact, there are those who make a living from judging and making up ridiculous stories about individuals. Judging comes easy to people in general. Some awareness in this field would be beneficial to us all. Every time we judge someone we are interfering with their natural way of being. Every time we judge ourselves we are belittling and decreasing our self-esteem. In whatever way we judge, it will always come back to us harming us.

When we are judging ourselves, we are denying who we are. We are sabotaging our potential and abilities, which could otherwise lead us to infinite possibilities. Our creativity and enthusiasm closes down on us and we find emptiness where there is supposed to be fullness, dullness where there is supposed to be excitement, nowhere to go where there are supposed to be great opportunities, depression where there is supposed to be joy and fulfilment, failure where there is supposed to be success.

We find it a challenge to stop judging completely because although we think we do not judge others, as soon as there is something in the news that is very contrary to what we stand for, our judgement comes up as if it were an arm ready to attack anyone opposing our beliefs. It is also easier and more pleasant to listen to someone who talks on a wavelength familiar to our own. Here we are not judging, but the sensations we feel listening define where we stand.

There are those who work hard in the spiritual way and think that they are free from judgement until they are surprised with the smallest thing, reminding them that they are still human and there is still a lot to learn and a long way to go. There are those who keep saying they do not judge but are judging as they speak, those who believe they have the right to judge others because they consider they know the true way of how things should be. We all think we are the ones with the truth.

Blessings fall on those who allow life to take them through unknown paths, surprise them at every sunrise, amaze them at every sunset, dazzle them by the beauty they encounter. Be grateful for all experiences no matter how challenging they may be. Love everyone. Care for everything. Respect the whole collective. Be thankful to be alive.

TRUSTING OURSELVES

T rusting ourselves does not mean that we do everything that comes to our heads, because quite often the thoughts we have are not even ours. So what do we understand by trusting ourselves?

Trust is free from doubts and gives us a feeling of security, which we feel comes from deep within us. With it there is a connection to a bigger spectrum that encompasses all we do and how we go about doing it. This makes us secure, powerful, calm and confident in what we say and do. This trust with which we speak and act sparkles light in others, who want to feel the same. It resonates trust within them too. If we lack this kind of trust, we will always be lost looking for something to satisfy us and not finding it. We may be deluded believing we have found it when we find something new, until the novelty disappears and we are back to where we started looking for something else. While having this strong trust in ourselves, we are sure of what we do, what we want and how to go about getting it.

Sometimes, out of the blue, a nagging feeling surprises us. It is like a very fine thread that makes its way through the tangle of nerves in our system and comes with a flavour of doubt without making us doubt exactly. It is so subtle that, unless we are very observant about how we feel and think, we would not spot it. This is enough to undermine our trust in ourselves and make us change aspects of our lives. So we need to pay attention with the eye of a hawk otherwise, without realising it, we could take wrong turnings on the road of life.

Another way we can change is by the company we keep, especially if they are strong-minded in what they believe. We will have to be stronger than them in order to avoid being influenced by them. The old Spanish saying, "tell me who you spend time with and I will tell you who you are" is appropriate in this case.

We notice with interest that we frequently come across situations when, unless we are awake and aware, we fall where we do not want to without realising we are falling. What can we do? Be alert, be aware and be calm. Go inside yourself and find out who you are. Invisible help will come to your rescue if you are in fear or doubt.

When we trust ourselves to the very core, there will not be fear or doubt; there will be a sensation of achievement even before we have reached our goals. When we trust ourselves we feel strong and nobody can move us from that inner force that, at times, can be so powerful that we take off in a reality we are not used to, even though it is our true reality.

The more time we spend there the easier it will be to accept it and enjoy it. The infinite truth never changes, although the ways in which it can be interpreted vary immensely.

RESPONSIBILITIES

When we are responsible for everything we think and do we are enhancing a balance in our surroundings, our community and the whole. This makes us feel strong and we inspire trust in others. We are open to wisdom and we allow it to work through us, giving us the opportunity to help those who come to us in search of support. The opposite happens when we blame everyone and everything for what happens to us and to the world. Somehow we always think it is someone else's fault. We may feel that we have nothing to do with what is happening around us and ignore our input in it by what we think, say, do and feel.

Our first responsibility is to keep ourselves in check because our influence determines the output we send out to those we live with, the community, the country and, in a subtle way, the whole world. It is well known that we can reach anyone at any time in any part of the world by projecting our thoughts. Our thoughts are charged with energy, and depending what type of energy we are sending, we could benefit or damage the target where we are sending it. This is a big responsibility to take as lightly as so many do. We will do well by examining what we think, feel and do, bearing in mind the consequences it can bring back to us, because all that we send out will come back to us in one form or another.

We see when the masses follow a particular thought that the results can be very damaging, bringing countries into conflicts and ending up in wars. Sometimes these disastrous situations start with only a few people. Their thoughts are so powerful that they are able to influence anyone who is not prepared for this kind of attack. They can very quickly recruit many followers. A word of caution: Who do we follow? Why do we follow them? How is that going to affect us, and what will be the consequences? Knowing the answer to these questions, are we still prepared to follow this path? The choice is always ours.

A lot of us may say that we are responsible for our families and our job. Some will go as far as their communities and then there are those who go worldwide and want to rescue the world from the damage caused by others. Often we will find that those very dedicated people have not spent any time caring for themselves. Therefore they are not being responsible for their own wellbeing.

It is quite noticeable when we are in the presence of a person who is responsible not only for a few things but also for everything. We feel a sensation of trusting this person, even if we do not know him or her. We feel comfortable and at ease in the company of such a person. We feel charged and connected. Our spirits go up. Our enthusiasm is high. We want to do things because our energy has had a boost that has lifted us to the top and makes us fly without limits.

Being responsible with integrity in this physical world can be a hard task for some. For others, it will be natural to follow their inner connection and allow the guidance given to them to live life in a responsible and safe way.

If we accept and value ourselves for what we are, if we love ourselves like no one else can, then we can be responsible for ourselves and consequently for our planet.

LOOKING FOR WHAT WE ALREADY HAVE

. . . .

We learn from different sources that all we want to know we already know. It is within us in a dormant state waiting to be awakened. This happens in many different ways to different people. There are some who do not want to be awakened and carry on sleeping.

The synchronicities in our lives make us curious. The religions we are born into also make us reflect on aspects of life. Even as children we ask questions, especially when we see contradictions and want to know more. However, there are many who will follow traditions already established and that is fine. We will focus on those who want to satisfy the thirst to know more, who will travel far and wide on the globe in search of knowledge and ways of acquiring it. They will meet new people who will give them new methods to use and they will apply them until the questions come up again. Thus they move on to a new group and try their ways of finding knowledge and applying it. Some will be satisfied. But others will keep asking the same questions. At the beginning, it all seems interesting and they are happy to learn. But when the novelty is over and the same questions come up, they know that their own way still has to be found. Thus the search goes on.

This group of seekers finds that the essence of what they have discovered is what they have always known, with differences in various practices they encounter that they are happy to practise themselves until they come across the same basic questions. Then they know those are not the ways they want to follow. Here, again, there will be those who will carry on looking for the answers in the outside world and others will go on looking inside themselves. This time, they will have conviction and trust in themselves, because now they know that all the knowledge they require and they will ever want is inside and they will never find it on the outside. That realisation is such a relief to them. They feel richer in many ways for having met so many people and so many paths to reach the peak of their objectives.

We have insights and synchronicities every day and sometimes they puzzle us. Other times we ignore them because they become familiar and habitual. Our imagination will take us into what we may think is a fantasy, but it can turn out to be a brilliant idea and that is a great way to expand and progress.

When we go to seminars or workshops and they do not give us anything that we do not know, instead of blaming the event or even ourselves, it helps to go inside and check the reason for still going to workshops. We may find we lack trust in our insights and lack confidence in ourselves to acknowledge what we know. We can still go for the pleasure of it and to meet up with people who think like us. It is comforting hearing others who are saying or doing what we have been doing and believing for a long time. And just in case we do not quite believe in ourselves, we get the opportunity to confirm that there are more people with exactly the same ideas and very often they use the same words to express them as we do. Have you found that sometimes you hear or read something that matches what you are doing and yet you started to do it without any input from anywhere or anyone? It came from your insights, your inner knowledge.

WE CAN CHOOSE

We start by choosing our parents. We choose them according to the experiences we want to have on this planet and the projection we want to manifest. After the age of five, or even before, many of us forget that we have planned the scenario we find ourselves in that we call life.

So, if we choose our parents, we are already taking on board the kind of life we are going to have and that is what we wanted to experience, learn from and expand beyond. Once we are in our chosen life, we may not like it or we may love it. It will all have to do with our choices. We have the privilege of manifesting anything we wish and that involves choices - choices that will determine the course of our lives. Even as a child we can decide what path we will take. We often hear parents saying things about their children like: *She is so musical and is singing all the time. He loves planes and wants to be an aeronautical engineer. She loves animals and wants to live on a farm. He wants to be a doctor, teacher, builder, etc.* Our projection starts to take shape with the comments we make and the interests we have as children. Our parents will do their best to help us to be in the field we want to be. Of course, there is another side to it. We may have chosen a family whose income is not going to allow us to be where we wish to be. This is where choices are important. As a child we know we can get anything we want by projecting it in our mind and allowing it to come about. However, challenges start when our parents or guardians tell us that we cannot do something and give us a whole list of reasons to prove it, which to adults make sense but not to children who know they can get anything they want. All kinds of things can happen and they will have to make do with the choices we make for them.

We are starting to understand that when we think about something with a vibration we manifest it. Even though it is happening to us, we still do not believe we can change our lives by the choices we make. Therefore we create our own problems and blockages, which then we have to find ways to overcome.

By forgetting that we are projections of a higher existence we get very tangled in the processes we find on the planet. Some of them may have been created to challenge us, thus giving us the opportunity of being involved in problem solving. Or we could be the problem creators. What we were not created for is to hurt each other. We always have the choice and it is through our choices that we govern every second of our lives. If we think about what we do from the moment we get up to the moment we go to sleep, we will see that we spend the day making choices, which are activated by our thoughts and then manifest what is in our minds. We sometimes manifest things and situations in our lives that we never wanted to have, and yet we do not recall having thought or chosen them. The choices of the collective affect us as well. Therefore, we may be in situations we had nothing to do with, but as we are a part of it through being connected to the whole, we suffer the same consequences.

The power of thought takes us where we want to be, even if it seems remote and impossible. The choices we make do the rest. Our adventures can be pleasant and fruitful or they can be real tragedies for all of us. So awareness of our thoughts and choices can make a difference to all of our wellbeing, our planet and us.

WE BELIEVE WE KNOW

Through constant changes we acquire certain likes and dislikes, which keep changing as well. We create habits and we stick to them, often without knowing why. In some people habits control their lives. Ideas come and go. Some of them we follow and others we don't. Have you noticed how our minds change? If we look back at our past years we will be surprised at the changes we have made, the things we are doing and could not have imagined being able to do. Our pitfall is to believe we know, because in reality we do not.

We believe our ideas are ours and only ours. Are they? So how can it be that as soon as a person has an idea, several others, from different parts of the world and without knowing each other, have exactly the same idea? Who was passing on the idea? Was it theirs or ours? Do we know?

We believe we know ourselves based on what we do. However, we never know how we would react in certain situations. We can say that if this or that happened to us we would behave in this or that way. Yet when it happens, we are surprised at what we do or say, and it is not at all what we had thought it would be.

We can go through life wanting to pursue a dream. Although there are opportunities, somehow they never happen. Although we think we know, we give ourselves endless reasons or excuses for it not to take place, when in reality we have not stopped and asked ourselves sincerely why it is not happening. Had we done so, we would have found out the real reason and would have done something about it. It does not have to be a dream; it could be the simplest things of day-to-day life we wish to do or have and yet do not seem to reach. That gives us a feeling of dissatisfaction and lacking.

We believe we know why we think as we do. But we have not stopped to ask ourselves if all the thoughts that come to our mind are ours or someone else's. We may feel strongly that our thoughts are ours, but if they were put to the test we would be surprised at what we might find. Those who really know are very careful not to run away with their thoughts so as not to be puppets for others, especially knowing that thoughts are the creators of the actions that will follow.

Some people follow habits which may make their lives difficult, and still they will not stop to ask themselves where they picked up that habit and why they are following it. They will tell you that they always do that. They believe they know.

There are those who strongly believe they know others well. But what they know is their habits and ways acquired through the limitations they impose on themselves. We cannot know others when we do not know ourselves. It is easy to look at the outside world and believe our own world is safe. We forget that we are seeing a reflection of what is inside our own world. Many do not want to know. Others are frightened of what they may find. But some will go in and deal with whatever they find.

When we believe we know, not only do we not know but also we close the doors to knowledge by blocking new information that could unveil the truth about who we really are. Seeing who we are would be a great step towards a better world.

OUR HIDDEN QUALITIES

. . . .

S o many of our natural qualities are hidden and we think we do not have them. We may see them in others, but not so easily in ourselves. When we do, we have a feeling of doubt that stops us from being spontaneous on occasions. We waste time thinking about it and it becomes a burden that takes up space in our mind and therefore we lose energy and opportunities from it.

There is a minority who know exactly what they want and how to achieve it. Their self-esteem is high and they believe in themselves. They have important missions to accomplish, which will help the rest of humanity or destroy it. Possibly, there will be individuals on both sides of the spectrum. Let us concentrate on how the majority of us find some of these hidden qualities.

There are two people who are doing a job together. Anne is the leader, who knows the job; Ben is the apprentice, who wants to learn and help Anne. (These are not their real names.) They used to meet up and travel together in one car. Ben was always early, because he did not want to make Anne wait. Anne was always late, very late, sometimes up to an hour. The first few times, Ben did not say anything. But as the days went by and nothing changed, Ben became annoyed and would be silent during the journey. One day, when Anne enquired about his silence, Ben let out his frustration for being kept waiting for so long. Anne listened to Ben's complaints and politely apologised to him, softly and compassionately. This same scene went on for months and Ben was getting angrier as the days passed, until one day, when he had been waiting in his car for Anne for more than half an hour, feeling the fury and anger rising in his chest so powerfully that it made him stop completely his horrible thoughts about Anne. Suddenly there was a stop in his system as he thought: "This cannot be happening to me, just for the sake of it. There must be a reason behind it". The anger disappeared. There was silence in his mind. For quite a while there was just that, silence. Then a word came to him in a very particular way. It was as if the letters were taking over his body and the sensation of the meaning was imprinted on every cell of his body. There was no way to express how Ben felt. The word was "PATIENCE". It hit him so hard that tears ran down his cheeks and he felt humble and grateful at the same time. When Anne arrived that day, Ben got into the car in silence and kept it up for a while. He was still emotional about his experience. Anne was surprised not to have the usual shower of insults thrown at her and enquired: "Are you OK?" The soft "yes" was almost inaudible, in contrast to the loud and critical habitual words of the past months. Anne kept looking at Ben. For a long while there was silence. Then Ben said softly to Anne "I'm sorry for being so rude to you. Thank you for the beautiful lesson I have learned through these long waiting times". With a kind smile, Anne said: "I knew you would come to understand". From that day on Anne was always on time. Ben asked himself "Why did I have to take so long to learn something that jumped out at me with so much power in an instant?" He asked Anne this question too and the answer she gave him was "Your message came when you were ready to receive it". It was so powerful to hear this from Anne.

We sometimes go through unpleasant circumstances to discover something valuable. This is why we would be wise to make everything that happens in our life work for us in a positive way, so we do not waste time fighting our ego. The quicker we learn, the quicker we can enjoy the fruits of our learning and the more able we become to deal with life and to help others on their way. It is important to remember we have everything within us already and if we want something very much it will come up when we are ready to receive it.

JOY IN THE HEART

. . . .

The joy we feel in our heart is powerful and without limits. It comes out like an explosion; at times difficult for us to control. It shakes our physical body. There are times when the gift of speech cannot verbalise what the heart feels so strongly. So some people will jump up and down, and scream or cry. It is an excitement similar to a huge fire provoked by a strong wind, which seems out of control. However, there are equally powerful outbursts of joy and the symptoms are not so explosive. A different type of fire drives them. It is an internal joy that manifests in a harmonious and powerful sensation as if we were taking off up into the air and could dissolve into the clouds.

Between those extremes of joy there are many more, with so many tastes and degrees, according to our personality and character. The purity of joy changes through the passage of time. There are still some who will keep that purity all their lives. The majority have forgotten that joy is one of the ingredients we are made of. Forgetting this is like being lost. If we forget we have something, it is as if we had lost it. Therefore there is that sensation in us of being lost and lacking. People create many things and ways to rekindle the joy in their hearts. Some of these ways are pushed by the natural joy that is repressed and forgotten in our hearts. Other ways can be by dramatising the abuses of society and its people. The worst of them are using all kinds of animals, including humans, to create entertainment and distorted joy.

There is so much knowledge in our world these days. There are so many people, groups and societies spreading the word of knowledge. And yet in the hearts of people its natural way of being is blocked. How can that be? How can there be those who will go to courses to get more knowledge about themselves and yet when circumstances call them to use that knowledge they stick to their old habits and behave in ways as if they had never been to any courses or had not had any contact with the knowledge? How can that be when those who attend seminars, workshops or debates talk as if they had understood and learned all about the topics in question, but when it comes to putting those ideas into practice in the real world, they go back to their old ways and beliefs? Worst of all, they instigate others to follow suit. How can that be? How can we sabotage ourselves in that way?

We are not claiming to be wrong or right; only asking: Do we know what we are doing? Do we know where we came from and where we will go after this earthly journey? Do we know why we came here in the first place? Do we know what that involves? Are we doing anything to find out? And if we know, do we apply what we know? These are important questions and the answers will tell us where we stand.

We have to remember those joyful hearts, which are always willing to help and vibrate through the universe the voices of immense love and wellbeing. Their joy carries the power of all nature in it. Nature plays a great role in the field of JOY. If we feel joy by looking at beautiful scenery, a flower, a tree, a river, a mountain or the sea, it is because we are connecting the joy they are offering us to our own natural joy, the joy we were born with and is always there waiting for us to notice. Being connected to our natural JOY is the most sublime sensation we could ever have.

DEALING WITH THE MIND

. . . .

D ealing with the mind is quite a challenge for anyone except the enlightened ones. The mind keeps jumping from place to place and it is a job to keep it still and on positive subjects without bringing in negative ones or those that certainly do not serve us. The mind can become obsessive and will not listen to reason.

Have you ever been in situations where you are determined to be silent or meditate, you put all your intention into this, and to your disappointment just the opposite takes place? It is a tiring business dealing with the mind, because it wants to have its own way at all times. It keeps some people from going to sleep by bringing up subject after subject. It is very canny. If we are not determined not to listen to it, it will find subjects to catch our interest. A strong will and strong determination will put it in its place, even if just for a while.

Our mind knows how to hook us through negative memories, since its tendency is to go to the negative side of things. By observing our own mind from the perspective of an outsider, we can stop it quite easily, especially when we cannot go to sleep. It will be the mind observing the mind and the running around will stop. It is a relieving feeling, if we have been fighting our way to get to sleep without success.

An untrained mind can cause unpleasant situations, and those who do not realise this suffer most. Our awareness of what the mind is able to do will keep us on the watch for any signs we can see. Then it is a question of using our tools to deal with it. One such tool could be the one mentioned above, which works especially well for that particular situation. There are many more, of course.

Many people are familiar with the recurring thoughts that keep going in circles with a tiring and depressing effect. We cannot tell these people to stop those thoughts, because they cannot do it just like that. They need to replace those thoughts with positive thoughts, happy thoughts that they can engage with to break the cycle. The mind wants to control. Our awareness can control the mind by just being aware and using the breath. The breath is the most powerful tool we have, the most efficient, and always to hand. Deep breaths will help, and there are certain techniques which will bring immediate change.

When we observe ourselves with awareness, we will discover that we are attached to the subject of our thoughts somehow, maybe in ways we cannot quite understand from where we stand. Nevertheless, these connections exist. By becoming aware of these attachments we open up a way to eliminate them, and that will give us more control over the mind, merely because if there is no emotional attachment the mind will lose interest in the subject. There are many paths to take to achieve this and there are many people willing and happy to teach us how.

Dealing with the mind is a very refined skill because the mind can take us to the highest peaks and can also drop us into the lowest pits. It can surround us with success or failure without warning. It can take us where we want to be, provided we know why we go there. It can give us joy or sadness but we have to know which we want. It can fool and deceive us as well as compliment us and make us feel high. Yet we will not be aware of its tricks. Working with our mind with care and awareness will keep us where we want to be.

ASKING WHY

· ·

Have you asked yourself why we are what we are: sometimes, frequently or never? Many of us have done that many times. Why have we chosen to be male or female? Why have we chosen our bodies to be tall or short, thin or fat, with disabilities or really fit and healthy? Why did we choose our looks and characteristics so that we can differ so extremely in every way possible? Why did we choose the parents we did? What did we have in mind? Why the great social and financial differences? What did we have in mind? What were our targets and strategies? Are we close to meeting them? Or are we lost in the entanglements of society and ignorance? Why are we so intelligent and able at what we do or so slow to grasp information? Why do we fail in performance? Why do we have such advantages over others or are we at the other end of the scale? Why can we move from the bottom to the top of society or fall from the top to the bottom? Why can we be such loving or hateful creatures? There are so many more whys left. The list is interminable. We can stop here and adjust it conveniently to our own state of being.

Life could become really interesting if we were to start looking for answers to the questions above. Quite a lot of people are doing just that, but there are so many more who prefer not to know. They prefer to be blind to what they may find and their excuse is "I am happy as I am and I don't believe in anything else". We respect the way they want to live their lives. How about the others who want to know where they came from and what for? They are the ones who are searching for the path which will take them to the answers and fulfil their lives.

How do we find the clues to the answers? Here diversity plays a big role because depending on our own individuality the clues will be equally diverse. There are great similarities. However, we still remain very different, even though we are so much the same. Even if we apply the same techniques, the results will never be exactly the same. Some differences can be very subtle and not easy to see at first sight. But they are there. Clues come up when we want them, when we are ready to see them and understand them, when we look out for them, when we question what happens in our lives and how we feel in the role we have chosen to experience. Yes, we have chosen, whether we believe it or not. We have chosen our parents and the place we were born. This is a good thing to remember when we feel lonely and there is no one who can understand us. Remembering this, we will feel deep comforting warmth that will take us to the next step. Clues are in front of us all the time and they present themselves in ways we can understand, so that different people, according to their perception and ability of reception, can receive the same answer to a question in different ways.

Our physical body is always talking to us and is a major source of information telling us what is wrong or right with us. When we don't listen to it, pains and aches or illnesses come about. Listening carefully to our physical bodies pays off tremendously. Our emotional bodies are also a valuable source of information to guide us along and let us know when we are doing the right thing for us or not. Listening carefully to our emotional bodies, we will be spared a lot of suffering and worries. Our mental bodies can twist things around in ways we cannot always see clearly. So being watchful can take us far into success or neglecting it can take us into a place we do not want to be. Let us be aware of our real true Self so as to have a smoother journey.

LOVE

ove: this word is overused to such an extent that it dances on people's lips, frequently making a sound totally unconnected to the source of real LOVE. How many of us know the real meaning of it? Also, how many of us use it without feeling it? How many of us distort and abuse it? And, how many of us live in it a hundred per cent or even reach a percentage where we feel its subliminal ecstasy?

The word "love" is used in our society mostly in the context of temporary things or situations. "I love...." is used instead of "I like ..." to express a higher degree of liking. Love is used as the opposite of hate. Love is used when talking about any subject but does not convey the "real" meaning of it. Love is used to show affection and care. The most used ways are to express a higher affection between people, family, friends or anyone else. We could extend it to the world at large and the whole collective, each of us in our own capacity of feeling for the subject of our love. There are people to whom the word "love" has an eternal meaning. There are those who see and feel real love in everything and everyone.

Probably the closest we get to feeling real love is when we are in love and all our senses are caught in it. It seems that nothing else exists but the strong feeling we have towards the object of our love. However, we do this by default. It just happens. We do not seem to have control over it and if it breaks up for whatever reason, those people are heartbroken. They suffer and find it hard to overcome their suffering. Falling in love can happen several times to us. But when people are suffering the break-up of one love, they cannot envisage the fact of loving again in the same way. Happily, we can. It has been reported that sometimes it is better and stronger the following times we fall in love. However, no matter how powerfully we fall in love and for how long we keep it up, it is still temporary. That first amazing sensation of owning the world in our hearts through the passionate love we feel is not for ever. We change constantly and as we get older our changes are stronger and become influenced by all the events which have occurred in our lives. Therefore, our vibrant love is influenced too. Very few can keep it alive all their lives. For most people it will turn into a very warm and affectionate feeling or a separation.

When we are in a situation where we feel completely transported and we are not aware of our physical body because it has dissolved, we are connected to the Real Love. When that happens we will not forget it. The experience is so powerful and empowering that we want to keep it forever, and in fact, knowingly or unknowingly, we have touched our own core, our own reality, our eternal Love. This feeling can be felt in contemplation, in meditation, in admiring a flower or natural scenery, watching children at play, watching nature in its great diversity, watching anything that is natural and beautiful. That includes when people are able to touch the same chords of Universal Love and be tuned in to them. When we can feel this kind of love, we know what real Love is.

Love is the key that opens every door and smoothes every upheaval, the magical ingredient that resolves difficulties and problems, the tool that will operate anywhere and in anyone to bring out the best results. Love is the light that will help us to know who we are and guide us through our journey. LOVE is the ingredient we are made of. Having forgotten about it has made us vulnerable and doubtful of our right to be ourselves. By finding love, we can be strong, regardless of the opposition we may encounter from those who are still walking in darkness and refuse any suggestion of change. Universal Love is the most powerful tool in the world.

FEAR - 1 -

. . . .

Fear has many aspects and can come up through many avenues, some of them unknown to us and often disguised with an overall shape and colour for us to fall for. Once inside, the battle starts. Most of the fear we may experience is injected into us by different means, used very skilfully. It would help if we were aware of it and removed it as soon as we felt it, or had a notion that it was approaching us. Of course, many times it takes us by surprise and we are left to deal with it as best we can.

Most children are fearless. Parents instil fear in them with their warnings of "if you do that you will hurt yourself". These warnings start at an early age, and increase as we get older. Even as adults those "ifs" are there, trimming our wings and limiting our potential. Many people only realise in adulthood the consequences of that fear, which acts as a brake to our natural way of being. This conditioning causes much damage.

There are the fears inherited by the history of the planet and by those that came before us and left trails of it everywhere. There have been those who have written about this fear and how they have experienced it. Most of us feel fear without knowing where it comes from. The fact is that there are always reasons for things to manifest and exist.

We are already wrapped up in those fears, without our direct intervention. We also have those fears we brought with us from previous lives on earth. Not all of us are aware of them, although many of us are interested now in looking into them.

There are fears with different flavours and degrees of content which we find in everyday life. They come from sources unknown to us, from other creatures on earth, from natural disasters, from other humans with whom we may have had contact or not, from colleagues at work, from close family, from those in professions which could alter the lives of many, and an infinity of others.

Fear is a very strong negative energy. It is lethal. It is the strongest tool people use to get what they want at every level of society, and even in families and close relations. Fear is used to achieve power over others, debilitating them and removing their identity. It happens at national levels as well as individual levels.

WATCH OUT! We can remove fear from ourselves and help others to do the same. A lot of us know how to change this negative energy into a positive one. There are many techniques and tools to do so. Some fears will be more stubborn than others. Be sure they all go. The important thing is to remember who we are. We are beings of Light, strong and powerful. When this is in place, life changes for us. We recover our identity and we can see with clarity our potential to contribute to the wellbeing of the collective and the planet. Regaining our power is the best we can do in our time in this physical world.

Let us REMEMBER, at all times, we are powerful beyond measure, and when our intentions are for the wellbeing of the whole, our power is limitless. Let us be sure we understand this well. By harming others, we are harming ourselves. It will all come back to us. So let us emit light and receive back a stronger, splendorous, luminous LIGHT.

FEAR - 2 -

. . . .

It is essential to be free from fear. It is a powerful energy, which will cause destruction, pain, and panic, paralysing many so they do not pursue what they most want. It is a tool used worldwide to control nations, groups, families and individuals. It is essential that we do not create fear in anyone. Many people suffer the consequences of fear. It only benefits the very few. By being aware and able to process it, we will be in a strong position to face whatever is presented to us.

Fear used to be instilled in children at a very young age. Adults would talk about an imaginary monster or animal or anything else to make children do as they were told. Naively, it was used as a game, and that was the start of fear in them. As children grow up, they are still subjected to fear. Some children realise that by using fear they can obtain what they want and they will use it on their peers. As adults, they will carry on using fear as a tool for their own benefit, regardless of the harm they may cause.

Societies at large use fear and bring crises to countries to gain power in every sense. However, it is essential to remember that no one can take our power unless we allow it. If you have already been disempowered, you can reclaim your power by processing the fear and calling back your power from wherever you left it or whomever you gave it to. Anyone can do this. If you do not know how to do it, find a reliable practitioner to help you.

A lot of us have had experiences of strong fears from childhood, which expanded as adults and became a problem in our lives. Some of us have dealt with fear without outside help by trusting in our inner power and knowing it is there and we can do anything, no matter how big it may be. As soon as we make that stand, we recover the strength we thought we had lost or did not think we had. We know we can face fear. Some of us had no knowledge or tools to deal with it, just the determination that we wanted that fear out of our system. So we made a stand to remove it and succeeded. In today's world it is much easier, because there are so many helpers, healers and experts on the subject, and the only thing needed is to be awakened to what our reality is and differentiate it from the illusion we are living. For some, the use of fear works well. Unfortunately, they forget that by being in an illusory world, all they do is temporal and there is nothing they can take with them when the illusion comes to its end.

Fear creates inhibitions and resistances that act as brakes in our lives. How many times have we wanted to do something and found excuses not to go ahead and do it? If we take a closer look at the real reason, we will find a hidden fear somewhere.

We would like to say to those who suffer from fear that fear is only in the mind. If you can convince your mind of the non-existence of fear, you will not suffer from it. It is the mind that dictates what you are thinking and what you are able or not able to do. Changing the programme can change that. The big difference here is that you are in control of changing what you want and the way you wish to be, instead of someone else being in charge. When we are in awareness, nobody can fool us. They may do so for a while. However, if we are alert, we will see signs from our real true Self, showing us that we are not following the right way and that the way we are following has a dead end.

Being in our centre and aware of our true Self will keep us on the right path and safe.

DIFFICULT SITUATIONS

How do we get into difficult situations? How do we find ourselves in them without warning or awareness? These situations can vary from domestic to social ones, work related and financial ones; plus others that we could be involved in.

A life without awareness leaves us open to many things we would rather not experience, but somehow we end up having to deal with them. The kind of individual we are attracts us into the life we lead. As children, we already show signs of what kind of world citizens we will develop into. However, we also change with the natural changes of the universe, and those changes can go either way, favourably or unfavourably.

We have to be very clear about the fact that we choose our parents and therefore that sets up the conditioning we are going to endure. We could end up in a rich family, a poor one, a professional one or any other. Our status in life will be decided from the beginning, however that can change through the years as well. Bearing all this in mind, can't we see that *we* have chosen those difficulties? Since our passage through this life is a projection, before we launched the project we already knew what conditions we would find along the way. A lot of us have forgotten that. There is a minority who remember, and some of them excel in doing the hardest work of all.

Our lives on earth can flow like huge rivers with well-defined paths, like small rivers that can be diverted, like springs always fresh and new. Or they may have stopped flowing, becoming ponds or lakes. Our lives can also be like oceans, enhancing everything there is, strong and powerful. If our strength and power is directed towards the wellbeing of the collective, then there will be great success for all. If it is directed only to benefit some, then we are doomed. We are failing. We would have been caught by the distortions of the senses, and the project we were trusted with fails by itself.

Those who want to control the world, and collect all the benefits by making the population their slaves, can endanger our lives. Their tactics are invisible. They target people and countries. They create chaos and then make people believe they are bringing the solution, which is a cover-up to achieve their own goals. By becoming aware of what they are doing, and by not playing their game, which is based on fear, aggression and deprivation, we can stop this. A coin has two sides. Power has two sides. People have two sides. What we are able to do depends on which side we are on at any one time. Awareness plays a great role in this. If we are aware, we will not fall into the trap in front of us. This awareness will alert us to the danger and we can make changes accordingly. The important thing here is to be brave and remember at all times that the Universal Intelligence supports us incessantly. Another thing to remember is that we are powerful beyond measure. Nobody's power can surpass ours, because we are made out of the same energy. It comes down to believing in ourselves before we believe in others, approving of ourselves before we approve of anyone else, and trusting ourselves before we trust anyone else. Knowing that, when we are confident in who we are and when we are secure in our true Self, those who want to change our behaviour will not succeed. We will instantly feel that whatever they want to inflict on us does not belong to us. It is not our true Self thinking or behaving and we will proceed to clear those unwanted energies. Should anyone feel difficulties in doing so, seeking help from enlightened ones would be advisable. We are the co-creators of our lives. The power of intention and the power of knowing who we are will always manifest in favour of our wellbeing.

WHAT WE KNOW AND WHAT WE DON'T KNOW

What we know and what we don't know is like a paradox and we are sandwiched in the middle. How do we know we know? And how do we know whether what we think we know is what we are supposed to know? How do we know if what we know serves us or not? And how much truth is there in all we think we know? Where do "known and unknown" stand in our day-to-day life?

It is fascinating to observe from a distance, where we cannot be hurt and can remain objective, the mixed knowledge that moves amongst human beings and the contradictions that go with it. Individuals are in a world of their own and think they hold the truth of whatever they say or do. In our perception of life, we hold our own truth. That is how we see it and there cannot be any way other than ours. We may follow ideas from others, learn from others, read the knowledge of others and listen to the advice of others, but we will conclude by mixing and matching all that into our own way of seeing our truth. That is what counts for us. So who knows what?

Society works with labels. Each one of us is under a label: politics, law, religion, finance, family, institutions, societies, foundations, health, education, rescue, travel, media, exploring, news, agriculture and others, plus all their ramifications. Some people say they wear several hats or are under different umbrellas, meaning they are under more than one label. We may have superficial knowledge of most topics, but we have to be specialists in our field for others to believe us. We would trust one another in each one's speciality if we did not have that hidden mistrust born by thinking "we know best".

We seem to know so much in so many ways, and yet we know so little about the basic things in our lives. For instance, do we know who we are? Do we know where we came from? Do we know why we were born in this or that country? Do we know why we were born in this or that race and brought up in a particular religion? Do we know how our physical, mental and emotional bodies work? Do we know how to attend to the needs of our bodies? Do we know why we think what we think and why we like what we like? Do we know what we are doing on this planet? Do we know? In fact, we do know but we have forgotten the knowledge and we relearn it again and again.

Being aware of what knowledge is will lead us away from making mistakes or misleading others into confusion and pain. Also by being aware of the purity of our hearts and how we react to the pretentions of others we will know how to avoid misleading information. Knowledge is power and it can help or destroy us. Acquiring knowledge and possessing it puts us on a platform of responsibility to help the planet and the collective. We are all powerful beings. We may have forgotten it but that does not mean we have stopped being powerful and knowledgeable. It is for us to discern what our knowledge is and how we want to use it successfully for the wellbeing of all.

DISCONNECTION

. . . .

We connect and disconnect constantly with/from people, things, situations or places. Sometimes we are aware and sometimes we do it automatically without realising what we are doing.

Disconnection, separation and detachment carry the strong feeling of something breaking up and not belonging. When we disconnect from ties that are hurtful or disempowering to us, we will regain our power and that is beneficial.

Some disconnections can cause a lot of pain to all involved, especially if they happen in communities or nations, because they involve many people being affected and thrown into all kinds of negativity. Feeling fear, anger, frustration and impotence are some of the important powerful negative emotions that occur. Let us bear in mind that those negative energies do not stay only where the disconnection is taking place. They travel around and through the whole planet like an epidemic no one wants to have. And yet we are all affected by it in one way or other.

The main reason for mankind to grow and self-develop is to connect with oneself. Disconnection is going away from the target. It is forgetting who we are and why we came here. It is forgetting that we all belong to each other and to the world. It is forgetting that we are made out of the same dough, even though it can take different shapes. It is forgetting that our time is short and precious if we want to reach the expansion that will take us all up to a higher dimension of existence.

When we connect with who we are, life becomes fulfilling and opens up a great diversity of infinite possibilities. Effort is not necessary. Intention and being connected to the Source of all creation is enough to make our dreams come true.

Why do people find the simplest of things so difficult to understand and even more so to believe? Why don't they try it out at least? There is nothing to lose and a great deal to gain.

For some, to be rich is to acquire terrestrial wealth, which is temporary, and cannot be taken with them when they are called back. For others, to be rich is to acquire wisdom and the wealth that comes from it, for they can take this wealth with them and carry it to all other lives they may have through infinity. The choice is always ours. Whatever we do or whatever happens to us, we are our sole makers. We make our life as it is or allow others to make it for us. Let us be aware. Connection to our higher Self brings wholeness and bliss.

CONNECTION

· ·

To be connected to the highest is what a lot of us aspire to. We all want to be connected to everything else. To be aware at all times of that feeling of connection with our world and what surrounds us gives us the feeling of belonging. It makes us sensitive to every vibration we come into contact with, and even if we are far away from what and where we are connecting with, we still feel it.

Some people can be as sensitive to a small stone as to a huge rock, to a daisy as to the most beautiful displays of flowers, to a tiny plant as to an enormous tree, to a beggar or to anyone else through the levels of society, to everything there is in the sky and on earth. That sensitivity is our connection. We feel connected. We feel the connection strongly if we are in our now, in our present moment. Our connection enhances all there is, everything and everyone becomes us. Some people can only get that connection through meditation, but we can have it all the time when we are present and aware. If our mind takes us away from our now, we become disconnected from what is around us. We may not even hear what has been said or we may distort the situation because of our absence from the present moment. When we are not present, we lose momentum in anything we do.

Being connected means that in our present moment we have access to everything we may wish will come our way. It happens in very subtle ways and that is why it is so important to be present in every second of our lives. All the time we are absent from our now, we are missing out. We can also get into situations that could have been avoided. Being connected is like being in a network that works for us automatically. It directs us to do something we would not even dream of doing, and yet is perfect and brings the right results for everyone. It happens in such subtle ways that it is hardly felt. Once it has taken place we let it go, even though our ego may wish to linger with the amazing feeling of achievement that would lead us to attachment and all its consequences. This connection is free from attachment. It is important to differentiate that. This connection gives us freedom while attachment takes it away. We can all do it. We all have access to the wonders of our natural network.

Waking up to the capacity of knowledge and the possibilities we carry with us at all times will give us the most exhilarating experiences, which we could not even dream existed. It would dissolve all the man-made problems and replace them with wonders. It would awake in us our natural and unconditional love, which will make us sensitive to all around us and through which our quality of existence will go up to the highest it can be.

For some of you, reading this will resonate within you. For others, you may find it far-fetched and impossible. However, the fact you are reading it means you have taken a step forward in the right direction to understand it and that will lead you towards ways of finding the answers you may be looking for. The thing to remember is that nothing is impossible and that the Universe has an abundance of anything we may want and beyond our wanting.

When we feel connected, we also feel we belong to everything and that everything belongs to us. When we look at the moon, we feel in the moon. When we look at the sun, we feel in the sun. When we look at a plant, tree or the sea, we feel in them as well. We are a special piece of the Universe.

BEING AT THE EDGE

We are always at the edge in everything we do. What we learn is the skill to hold on safely to the wheel of life and navigate at ease so as not to fall from the edge. Our job is to keep the balance, manage the movements and be in alignment with who we are.

There is a big difference between understanding the above and living it. Situations can be so delicate, so intricate, that they pull us to the very edge, where we feel the vertigo and the fear of it. We are surprised to find ourselves in these situations, even when we can be the ones alerting others to be careful of the fall. It happens surprisingly fast and without us noticing it. It feels almost as if someone else is giving us the push. To avoid falling is to be in control and in our centre.

Being at the edge we have so much knowledge to enjoy. However, there are many distractions that can take our attention from it. The unexpected can come our way and we will react, attracted by the prizes the distractions offer. Here is where we lose our equilibrium and we may fall, unless we rapidly gain control. These experiences will show us where we are and how far we can stand by what we know. It will also measure our strength and capacity to hold onto the reality and not go with the illusion.

Have you been in situations where, after falling for the bait, you question yourself by asking, 'Why and how did I manage to do that?' It seems so ridiculous and out of character, but we did it. The feeling that comes afterwards is devastating and we would wish it would go. It will go if we accept it as a lesson and we learn from it. It will stay if we feel uncomfortable about it, because we are holding it with that feeling.

Being at the edge feels good, especially when we are in control and know what we are doing. When we are well aligned to the Universe we can take great risks, which will give us momentum, excitement and fulfilment, as well as the immeasurable pleasure of being ourselves, free and happy.

Being at the edge is like flying a plane by yourself, with the difference that the plane is tailor-made for you and you are the only one who can fly it. The heights are threatening and at the same time daring. They are challenging and inviting. They are pushing you to the very edge, where your real power takes over and does the rest.

What would you do if you were at the edge of a precipice and any slight movement would make you fall off? Where would your attention be? Would you be thinking of your friends? Activities? Food? No, of course not. In the same way, by keeping our attention on everything we do with that intensity, the outcome of our days are brilliant and successful at all times.

We are grateful that we are given these opportunities to excel and use our abilities to do so.

Being at the edge keeps us alert and focused, wanting to learn more and embrace life with a difference, the difference of feeling success surrounding us and the joy of making us feel vibrant.

WHEN WE DECEIVE OURSELVES
AND BELIEVE WE ARE IN THE TRUTH

When we think we are living a reality and find out it is far from it, this carries unexpected connotations. Deceiving ourselves thus is long and painful, impossible to understand. And yet it is often hidden to such an extent that we live with it without knowing that it is there. The adversity of this condition drives us beyond ourselves, but somehow we stick with it, standing by the inner guidance of being true to ourselves.

It is amazing how many difficult situations we face in life and how well we endure them. We may dislike them as we live through them, but they make us strong and able to do the job we came to do. However, it is not always easy to see it like this. It is when the whole picture comes to light that we are able to realise the complexity of the game we came to play. Sometimes it is enjoyable. But when we are lost in it, it becomes really hard.

If we look attentively at all the minute details of our lives, we will see how well programmed they are: not a detail is missing. We will observe that by living our lives the way we do, we may make detours in the process, delaying the learning. These delays may lead us into more difficulties, which in turn will produce the greatest lessons of all. They happen by using our freedom of choice or the illusion of it.

It could be that life will take us to the very end of our tether, and in our exhaustion we will not see the path to follow any more. It is there we pause and assess what is happening to us. We look for options but find none. We may find ourselves in a standstill time-space situation without any exit to be seen. What do we do? Who can help us out? We learn and learn non-stop. We will find people with good will, keen to advise us but our heart tells us that the advice given will only work for those who give it. We have to find our own remedy by ourselves. That realisation is hard to swallow, because in a psychological way it leaves us with the feeling that there is no support for us. There is nowhere to find answers, if the answers are all inside us. There is no one to turn to but ourselves. We may choose to waste time by feeling lonely and lost for a while, until our senses clear up and we go back to our centre with a different attitude. Now it is time to go deeper into ourselves and find the juice we were missing all these years. By doing that, we immediately connect with the inner guidance, which smoothly leads us to where we are supposed to be. The sensation of wellbeing runs through us, as if saying, "it is OK: all is well", and we carry on to the next stage of our lives stronger and with more determination.

When we reach that part of our lives and look back on all the years we have lived, it is like a puzzle where all the pieces fit into place and we can now see the real whole picture. We are in awe at how we could go through so much and have managed to do it all. It is then we realise we are more than just a physical body. We have such capacity for enterprise, in so many different situations, no matter how difficult they may present themselves. We can do it. We can always do it. Let us bear in mind that we can move forward through any situation we may encounter in our lives.

A piece of the puzzle to remember to put in place is the piece which seems hidden from us. Asking ourselves questions we will find the answers. Then we will see that the signposts have been there all the time but we were not awake enough to understand them. Let us all wake up and know that what seems to be is not always what it is. Let us enjoy the awakening to our true selves.

COEXISTENCE

· ·

Living together has many challenges, starting at a very personal level of family, community, region, country, continent and the whole world.

Society today has many more inhabitants, cultures and religions than in the past. So we need skills to adapt, share and support whatever we believe in, and in whatever way we wish to express it, provided we respect the code of conduct established by nations to keep the peace and wellbeing of all the citizens of the world.

We would be wise to start by learning how to live with ourselves, because there are many cases where the real problem starts by being strangers to ourselves and not knowing how to deal with who we are. This can create the basis of future unrest around us, which will then spread to the rest of our surroundings and, like a tsunami, will affect large areas.

Being aware of our identity, honouring and being grateful to our parents who helped us emerge on this planet, respecting who we are, and being curious about why we are here and what we came to do, all this will put us in a space of wonder. This is a good place to be because it takes us into the core of who we are. From there, we will learn what really matters and will see the real Self who, far from creating trouble and suffering for ourselves or anyone else, wants to be heard and understood. If each of us had these concerns, we would be able to live together and be happy.

Living together has a lot to do with how we live with ourselves and what kind of relationship we have with the person we think we are. The background we have chosen to come into will be predominant in how we will be thinking, although that can throw us one way or another. Time and again, what we end up doing does not resemble in any way where and how we were brought up. Maybe it serves us as a challenge to navigate towards our goals. Challenges are there for all of us, no matter how rich or poor we are, no matter how intelligent and able we are compared to those who appear to be different. We all have our challenges to deal with. The important thing to remember is not to put ourselves above or below anyone else, because in the real world we are equals. That knowledge alone gives us the strength and power to face any challenge we are presented with. This is why it is of major importance to know how to live with who we are.

Some have a gift for influencing people. Others have a gift for following someone with ideas because they are asleep and unaware, so they cannot see that they can also have ideas. Whichever we are, it is good to keep asking questions. We may find greater ideas than the ones we are dealing with now.

Having managed to resolve how to live with ourselves, living with others will be easy. By conquering ourselves, we are conquering the world. Being our true selves will put us in a space from where we can see how to manage living in a family, community, region, country, continent and the world. Our harmony with other people will not be based on how they look, what they believe, if they are rich or poor or where they come from. We will see them all from our real true Self, because that is where we are equals and there is nothing to fight about. All we see is an ocean of love that merges us and brings us together. Have you ever felt that feeling?

PATIENCE

P atience is a virtue which unfolds in thousands of ways, beautiful for third parties to observe, because we can see the effects of it without being involved directly and it stands out impacting the observers.

As babies and small children we have to be patient with our parents or those who take care of us. They may do things to us or want us to do things that we are completely against. Since we know we cannot stop them, we simply use the great virtue of patience, allowing them to make many mistakes on our behalf. Parents are presented with situations where patience is the only way out, so they are also patient, and it is a blessing for them to have that quality of patience awakened in them.

Vocational doctors, nurses and carers display such a degree of patience that we can see straight away if the person we are dealing with is a vocational professional or simply someone with a job they are being paid for. Vocational professionals speak with a softer voice. They look at their patients with interest that comes from the heart. They are concerned and genuinely want to help. They will do their very best for the people they are trusted with. They will explain the best they can in order to be understood by those in their care. They will reassure them with infinite patience and make them feel good about themselves. On the other hand, those who are there just for the money are a different kind of fish and patience is absent from them in a very noticeable way.

Another important sector where being vocational makes a huge difference is education. A vocational teacher can make students who do not want to study reach their highest capacity, whereas those for whom it is just a job will lose even the most gifted students. Teachers who do their job as a vocation are passionate about the subject they teach, so they infect their students with their enthusiasm. Their patience in teaching and dealing with students with difficulties stands out.

Patience pays off in prisons. If officers are patient with the prisoners, they will inspire the discipline and behaviour they want without resistance and many unfortunate situations can be avoided.

Many jobs that relate to serving the public would benefit from this ingredient: PATIENCE.

The observer sees in patient people calmness and a connection to whoever they are dealing with, which is admirable and touching. The tone of their voices, their body language, their approach, their patience, and the look of love and compassion in their eyes makes one feel that there is someone who not only cares but is making sure something will be done to make the patients feel better.

Nature as a whole is patient and we would do well if we took time to learn from it.

Patience is a beautiful sensation that comes from us, radiating from our loving heart. It can be seen the same way we see the moon when it reflects the light of the sun. It is visible and you feel it leaving a trail of wellbeing. Who is patient in your life? How does that make you feel? Are you patient?

KNOWING HOW TO BE

. . . .

As each wave of the ocean is aware of all the other waves and its water belongs to the whole ocean, the same is true with us. We are all made from the universal consciousness and belong to the same ocean of light, the difference being that not all of us are aware and therefore we create disharmony.

Knowing how to be is a topic that would take us hours to discuss and we are not going to deal with it here. So let us look at some simple aspects of it. For example, some of us have reached a level of knowledge which allows us to see through and beyond others, and that is fine. It is when we see how easily a problem or situation could be solved or avoided that those with the knowledge have to know how to be at all times: how to behave, how to hold back from giving advice, and how to keep a neutral ground, unless of course they have been asked for help, in which case, they will do their best to help in whatever capacity they can. All that is fine provided the helper is not intruding into the capacity of the helped and thus stealing their power. This can happen easily by the zeal of the helper wanting to help and forgetting that we are all helpers. In the same way as helpers are helping those who have asked for help, so also the helped are giving the opportunity to the helpers to perform as helpers. Consequently, they are providing a platform for the helpers to act. In so doing, the helped become helpers too. With this knowledge in mind, compassion and love are at work and, most of the time, they are sufficient to solve all kinds of problems.

Some may feel they know it all and that only they know how to do something. These are the ones who will help without being asked and will not see that their help is not needed or wanted. Observing the situation and the people involved in it carefully will give a full view of what we can do or not do. Sometimes we see very clearly how easily a situation can be solved, and yet, that is not what is needed or even appropriate for those affected. It has been known for "good intentions" to create turmoil or worsen a problem. What is needed is an awareness of where we stand and what our role is in that precise moment.

Knowing how to be presents a challenge for those whose knowledge tells them how to go about helping others and eliminating suffering or lack of alignment. They have to refrain from action because they are not free to move into other people's lives solving problems. These were designated for those other people to solve as part of their own learning programme even though they may have forgotten about it. We are at a point in our existence where only we can be our own saviours. However, when situations are such that help is asked of us, then we are free to give it as part of our own programme.

It can be hard when we live with loved ones and they have illnesses that we know we can help with, but they do not ask for that kind of help. So we cannot do anything at all, apart from watch them going to see the doctor to be prescribed more drugs which do not always work. The problems remain.

Knowing how to be is as important for us as for those around us. Often we can help more by standing back and doing nothing than by putting ourselves where we are not supposed to be. Knowledge and awareness will guide us to the right way to conduct ourselves. It is tricky sometimes - usually when our ego is at work. Knowing how to be will depend immensely on how much awareness or ego we have.

TIME

. . . .

For many of us, time is important in so many ways. How do we manage to be caught by this concept of ours about time? We all have our own ideas about time. Nevertheless, we all experience some elasticity in the notion we have of it. When we are busy every hour of the day, especially doing what we enjoy, time goes very fast, to the point that we do not see the weeks pass us and suddenly it is New Year again. However, time can drag if the opposite happens and the minutes are so long that they stretch to give us the feeling of being hours.

Time slows down for us when we are waiting to see a doctor, waiting in airports for delayed flights or in stations for delayed trains, waiting to meet someone who is running late, waiting for an answer that will change our lives, or when we are doing a job we dislike. The list goes on. On the other hand, the opposite happens when we are having a good time, for example: holidays, time off work, being with those we love, being in a job we enjoy, when we manage to fit everything in the right slots, in short when everything goes well for us. There are so many situations when the elasticity of time is remarkably visible. Have you ever been on a flight where you feel it is taking a long time and the hands on your watch do not seem to move? Or, have you been seated next to someone with whom you had the most interesting conversation and you arrive at your destination without having been aware of the journey? Time just went without you realising it. Our sense of time can expand or shrink without us being aware.

So what is time? Does it exist or do we make it up? How is it that most of us are controlled by time? All our technology works with very precise timings. We can get lost talking about time and we would not quite understand it unless we went to the very depth of who we are and what we are doing here on planet earth.

The experts tell us that time does not exist and some of us would agree with that concept. Have you ever mixed up the timings of a visit, meeting or event? Some of us have. Arriving at a house where you were invited for dinner, dressed up for the occasion, you found your host as he opened the door, lost for words and dressed in casual clothes. When he finally found the words he said, "the dinner party is tomorrow". Have you ever felt that sensation of being lost in time? A feeling of emptiness in the stomach and wanting to run away, but your feet are glued to the ground? These strange sensations can linger with you for hours, sometimes days. Other times, we may turn up to an appointment hours before it is scheduled. Worst of all is when we are looking forward to an event, and when we arrive at the venue we find out it has taken place the day before. Having anticipated the pleasure of the event for weeks, we feel devastated. Again, it is a feeling of being lost in time. If anyone wants to make things better by talking to us, it has the opposite result. It is better to allow time to come back to our perception of it and from there we carry on in the illusion of time.

Those who travel through time lines have a better understanding of what time is. They keep telling us that time does not exist and that past, present and future are all one. When we are in the past or the future we are missing our present, which is the most valuable to us, since the projection we are in revolves around the now, this moment in time, not yesterday or tomorrow. The importance of our lives is in the present moment, what we are doing and how we feel about it. Worrying about time will take us out of it. By being mindful of the present moment we are in ourselves and therefore in this now.

WORK - 1 -

Work is essential to keep our faculties stimulated, for our personal growth and that of the world at large. Work brings expansion, prosperity and changes for everyone. It opens up new worlds and new ways to live our lives. In a practical way, we work to earn money to pay our bills. A minority of people work for pleasure. Each individual has his or her idea of what work is for him or her. Looking into it we will observe that no one does the work the same way, even when they are performing the same job. There are always exceptions, but mostly we will apply our own personal stamp to what we do, even if it is the way we handle instruments or measure things. At times, the differences could be so small that they would be unnoticeable to the naked eye.

A lot of people look at work as a necessity to survive and, provided they earn enough money to cover their needs, they are happy even though the jobs may be hard or dreary, dangerous or with an element of risk. On the other hand, there are those who carefully choose jobs which will satisfy them and bring in the necessary income to support their families. Then there are those who will go directly to their vocational job. These will be the happiest, doing what they love and what fulfils them, because their job is what they most want to do and they are dedicated to it. They will give their all to it and the results will be brilliant. Said simply, when we do what comes deep from within, we will always excel in whatever we do.

When we go to work with joy in our hearts, grateful for the new day and what it will bring us, that puts us in a state of harmony with what is ahead. That is a kind of determination that will balance all the odds and we will end up having a good day. When we set out excitedly for work, following our inner guidance and prepared for any results, good, not so good or excellent, then the day will be great.

For us to be happy in what we do, we have to put our input in by either feeling it in a natural way, as above, or by visualising our day at work as we would like it to be. If colleagues or bosses are difficult to work with, that is how they are and we do not want to be affected by their energy. If the situation becomes difficult, it is time to look for another job. Jobs will turn up, if we are open to them. It is when doubts creep in that our minds take us to negative scenarios of lack of vacancies, and doubts about us being at the level and capacity that the jobs require. Then we will struggle. We only have what we co-create for ourselves. We are the only ones responsible for what happens to us. We have the power to change things around but have to believe in ourselves.

It does not matter what our job is. Whether we are a rubbish collector or a great well-known genius, our job is equally important to society. Just think for a moment: if any jobs were without people to do them, what would the consequences be? Every job is honourable, no matter what it is. Every job is a part of the puzzle that makes up society, and without it the puzzle would not be complete. Missing that part of the puzzle would create imbalance and the other pieces would be at risk of falling apart. This is a reminder of how important our jobs are, no matter what we do. If we are not happy in what we are doing, we can change it. We can study or learn other skills. In today's world, we are lucky to have great facilities for studying via the internet at a very moderate cost, sometimes even for free. All it needs is our awareness of where we stand and what we want. We spend most of our time at work, so we can make sure that it is time well spent and gratifying to our senses, giving us a healthy disposition and awareness of how and where to be.

WORK - 2 -

• •

t is through work that the whole dynamics of the world move, and we move with it. Without financial means, we depend on our work. Our income, quality of life and satisfaction depend on the type of work we do. No matter at what level of society we are, we are all important contributors to the world and how it functions.

When people feel dissatisfied with what they do, it is time for changes. Asking questions clarifies the field. What do you do? How did you come to do that? Are you well prepared for that job? Is the responsibility too much or not enough? Do you love what you do? Do you enjoy doing it? Is there something else you would rather do? Are your colleagues a problem? Is your boss a pain to work for? Are you not paid enough for the job you do? There may be other issues that interfere with your job: health, family or others. There are always ways to get what we want in life. Sometimes it takes longer, but with determination and trust in ourselves we can find the right way for us.

Some people may find themselves going through difficult times due to a variety of things and that will lower their energies. If they are not alert and aware, this will cause them stress, depression, anxiety and generally feeling low. If they are not careful, they can get into a cycle of energies that will control them and they will feel unable to pull themselves out from that cycle. When people find themselves in this kind of situation, they feel lost and unable to discern what is what. They lose their sense of wellbeing and do not seem to know what they want any more. They feel the weight of those negative feelings pulling them down and find themselves exhausted and lacking clarity of mind, so are not able to make coherent decisions to move forward. They feel lost and anxiety comes over them.

It is very important to know that we co-create our own life through what we think. It is equally important to know that the vibration of our thoughts attracts other vibrations that will match them. Therefore, if we are thinking negative thoughts we will be attracting more negative vibrations from other people who are also having negative thoughts. This will amount to an enormous increase of negative feelings in us, pulling us down deeper. We are connected to that negative vibration and it is much more than we can cope with. However, knowing that our vibrations attract other vibrations that are the same, we are in a position to change our thoughts and hence our vibrations. It is in our hands to change. We have the power to do it ourselves.

We can always change everything. If we have doubts, excuses or buts, they are the product of lack of responsibility, fear or resistances that are holding us back. All of it can be dissolved.

We can change our lives. We have the power to do it ourselves. For those who feel nervous and do not know how to do it, support may be needed to begin with. There are many professionals with different approaches who are happy to help.

Being happy is in our nature, and even when we cannot see it, that attraction towards unconditional love and happiness is reminding us of who we are. Remember we can change our life with our thoughts. We are powerful beings!!

DISTRACTIONS

Being distracted is the cause of many of our errors and drawbacks. Distractions range from being minimal to being enormous and difficult for us to deal with. Distractions come in many forms and reach us in all kinds of ways. Mostly we are not aware of them until it is too late. Often people play games and intentionally distract us to create situations for their own benefit. However, it is up to us to be careful about what we do and how we feel doing it.

We could get lost writing about different types of distractions, because there are so many, so we will only touch on this subject a tiny bit. If we were to list the kinds of distractions we encounter in our day, we would be surprised at its length.

The most ordinary distractions are when our mind is focusing on what happened yesterday or what is going to happen tomorrow or in an hour's time. Our present moment is neglected and anything can happen in our absence from our now. Thoughts are invading our mind constantly and not all of them are ours, which is a double distraction. Being worried is an element of distraction too. Fear is the biggest of all distractions because of its paralysing effects. Manipulators of people and the world use it extensively. Some individuals distract others in order to get their way or to make sure a deal is to their benefit. We see how whole countries are distracted into situations, which take the attention of the population away from what is really happening.

All distractions need attention, but particularly those that are almost undetectable and which we can only see when we really know ourselves well and are vigilant as to what happens to us and how it happens. For that, the mind has to be clear and in the present moment. It is very subtle. That is why it can be undetectable for many. Those who sieve their thoughts and feelings as they come in will find it easier to spot as a pattern takes shape. We may be in our peaceful space when a feeling comes in that we know is not ours. First we are curious and allow it to be in order to see where it goes and why it is there. That is fine. The problem can be if that distraction has a negative charge and gets to us. It may have an attractive component that pleases us. We allow it in even more. This is the moment to allow or stop it. We can be with it for this one time. When the same thing comes again, we can see the pattern, and if we are intuitive we can even see where it comes from. It is vital now to stop it completely, otherwise our mind will be controlled by outside energies not ours. There are individuals who can inject ideas and feelings into other people's minds and then control them. For that reason and to avoid these distractions we would benefit from self-development in order to know ourselves better and be empowered at all times.

There are many ways we can work on our self-development. We can choose the one that suits us best. If we need help, there are lots of practitioners ready to help and guide us in any field we may choose. Regardless of which path we take, MEDITATION is the key to them all. An open mind helps to move forward faster because it is not restricted by old ideas and limitations.

If we meet with doubts of any kind, they are only blockages that need to be removed or dissolved. This is easily done. We just have to remember what we are. What are we? We are pure Universal Love. Sometimes we forget that. Clearing layers of unnecessary baggage accumulated through the years will bring us closer to feeling it.

TODAY

· ·

Today is a magnificent day. Today I am going to make my day vibrate with the force of life the Universe generously gives us at each instant, continuously. Today I am present. I keep my mind on the richness of each second and look into the face of infinity. Today I bring the walls of distortion down and see the sky with its brilliant stars shining. Today I am grateful for being alive, being who I am and being where I am. This is the right place for me.

I know that whatever happens today it will be up to me to make it happen. I am the only engineer of how the pieces of today are going to fit to give me satisfaction and fulfilment. No matter how many people are around me, no matter what my circumstances are, I am still in charge of today and every day. Other people, of all kinds, are always going to be there. There will be those who will want me to be as they wish, imposing demands on me from different angles: job, family, friends, society, and the government with legal requirements. In the past, I have given them all of me and have not found myself in any of it. Today is a different day.

Today I retrieve all my energy from different places, whether I have given it voluntarily or it was taken without my knowing and therefore without my permission. Today with all my pieces back I can see more clearly. The path opens up in front of me. I see an abundance of opportunities inviting me to take them. I feel free from the ties of the past pulling me everywhere and sucking me into others' wishes. Now I am free. Now I feel free. Now I belong to the whole.

At times I might have felt that giving in to others was the way. My heartfelt generosity gave and gave to the point of losing my identity. Who was I? I did not know any more. I asked my heart for help and I was amazed to find that all I needed was just in there, to hand. A great relief came over me and I made haste to connect with my real me.

Today the world looks different to me because I have made changes about how I want it to be for me. I made changes to what I want to happen in my life. In turn, by being me, I am giving more than before to everybody else and to the world. The ripple effects of these changes are already helping others in the same situations. The frequency of the energy travels at the speed of light according to the experts.

Today is a loving day that I want to share with everyone. Today is making a difference in my life. Today I can see the distortions I created for myself and then blamed on someone else. I am grateful to have reached the point of awakening that allows me to see what is and not what seems to be. By feeling the pinch, it has brought me to where I am now, living my day as if there were no other day, which could give me the chance of rectifying my conduct, thoughts or feelings. It makes the perspective very definite and poignant in a way that cannot be ignored.

I have expressed what today is for me in this magical wheel of life where, by feeling at the edge of the wheel, I am going to be more careful not to fall into the emptiness of no return and therefore pay more attention to each instant lived with my presence in it. Days come and go and it is up to me to stay awake and alert in order to maintain the momentum and enthusiasm found in TODAY.

KNOWING HOW TO LISTEN

. . . .

When we know how to listen to ourselves, the information we obtain is clear, free from interferences or distractions of any kind. Knowing how to listen means we are connected and the insights that come to us are reliable.

Because of the great activity of the mind and the non-stop thoughts reaching us or created by us, at times we can be confused as to what is real or not. Other times, we are not even aware of this fact and lose ourselves in the madness and entanglement of thoughts. This can lead us to take wrong paths, say wrong things and be in the wrong company according to the moment in time. In these conditions we do not see our choices or options because the exterior stimulus takes over, making us believe we are having a fabulous life, when all we are is out of sync, disconnected from our real base and our real true Self.

Knowing how to listen to ourselves is a skill that we all have integrated in our make up, in what we are. It is part of our package on this journey. It is up to us to use it or not. There will be some people who cannot feel it or make sense of it. That does not mean they do not have this skill. It means that they have not looked for it. They are not interested in it because the attractions to hand satisfy them more. They have not found out yet that the life they are living is just an illusion created by themselves, through which they have to find their reality, their true selves. If we tell them this they will laugh and treat us as lunatics. That is one of the ironies we come across. Here also comes a challenge for us. Do we believe and join them? Or are we true to ourselves holding the real truth? If we are, we are also holding the divine power within us.

There are many of us looking for that truth with genuine interest and we often find ourselves misled or lost. That discourages us in our search and we may give up or stop looking for a time, until a bolt of lightning will strike us into moving again towards our goal. Asking others is not always the solution, for we all have different ways of seeing, approaching and experiencing things. Therefore, we may be hitting the wrong rock following what others do, which works perfectly for them, but not necessarily for us. Caution is important here. Trying others' techniques may give us the sensation we are doing it right, because we do feel certain feelings within us. No matter what we feel, it will not compare to when we are in our own field with our own tools. There are many tools. Each of them has to be shaped to the job it is meant to do and also to the person who is using it. This is why we are going to work better and feel more satisfaction if we work with a tool which has been designed and made for us. We access the right tool by listening to our true Self.

Knowing how to listen to ourselves is of major importance, since we are listening to who we really are and we are tapping into the Universal Source of all there is. We will look at our life and we will see that it is a projection made by us, in time and space, like many other projections we have made and many more we will make. This physical body we chose will last the duration of the project (or call it journey or lifetime). Then our real true selves will get rid of the physical body to go back to base and start again with another projection. While it is good to live in the physical world experiencing what it offers, it will be beneficial to us to bear in mind that although it is good to live through the experiences as if they were true, nevertheless they are not true. They are the illusions we chose to experience. By taking the experiences seriously, we suffer through them. By bearing in mind the fact that they are not real, we approach life and what it offers with enlightenment.

THE JOY OF LIFE

Life is joyful and we decided to come and live with joy in our hearts. This can be contradicted by many because of the pain caused at our arrival in the majority of cases. Lack of control of ourselves and what parents or guardians inflict on us as babies, children and adolescents can vary drastically if born in a rich or poor family, or if the family is educated or uneducated, if it has alcohol or drug related problems, or other characteristics not well regarded by society. Also, the country we are born in, with all its traditions, history and religion, is part of what we will be brought up with. So even before we arrive on the planet there is a lot waiting for us, which could benefit us or handicap us. For some the question could be: where is the joy of life?

Regardless of the circumstances we may find on our arrival, the goal is to be happy no matter what. The first thing we do is choose our life, our parents and the country we are going to live in. So we know what to expect. Nobody inflicted a hard or difficult life on us. We chose it to be like it is. The questions to ask are: Why did I choose this life? What am I supposed to learn from it? Who will benefit from my life and in what way? We can continue to ask questions until we receive the answers that will show us the joy we are.

The joy of life is what we are in reality. Ignoring it will put us in a precarious situation, because if that joy were not acknowledged in us, it would be like having it switched off with no access to it.

The JOY of life is the monitor light in us that is always on. It expands and contracts according to the stimulus in our senses. We connect best with nature, because unlike humans its naturalness is permanent and we can connect with it easily. Everything in nature reminds us of the abundance of joy. Nature's beauty gives us a flow of joy that is essential for our existence. Walks in nature are beneficial to our wellbeing. With music we can also be transported into realms of joy. When we fall in love we are on top of the world. Two hearts have connected with the light of joy.

As observers we will find different tones of joy in society. We can find a lovely expression of joy in a beggar and a contracted one in the rich couple passing by. We see the joy of giving in someone who does not have enough to eat for the day but will share it with someone else, while those who have plenty may refrain from giving. There is no joy in their hearts.

Joy is contagious! When we have plenty of joy, we emit it around us for everyone to benefit from. It works like kindling when we pay a compliment, praise work done and notice qualities in others. Being joyful connects us easily to other people and interactions are smoother and more effective at all levels.

The joy of life is in each cell of our physical body, reminding us that is what we are. Being silent will bring these observations closer to home and we will notice much more our heart singing for no apparent reason. Our mind follows suit by looking at the things that bring joy to the heart. All our tendencies are focused on bringing joy into our lives. Whether knowingly or not, the objective of our coming here was to be joyful and bring the joy of life to others by reminding them that it is all around us, in the air we breathe, the water we drink, the sounds we hear, the beauty we are.

WORDS

There are so many languages filled with words for us to express ourselves with. Yet we find ourselves very often lacking the right words to express exactly what we want to say. Saying we cannot express it with words leaves a vacuum within us.

Words can do innumerable things for us. We can express our different moods in many ways and tones. We give orders and compliments. We lie and accuse others of what we have done ourselves. We play the victim in search for pity. We can glorify or destroy people, betray those who have been kind to us. We can write books, be good orators and move people deeply. We can make people laugh or cry, igniting in them feelings that will change their lives. We make promises and perhaps break them. We are polite or rude, refined or ordinary and vulgar. We teach and learn. The list is never-ending.

When we wish to express an experience or emotion really deeply and cannot find the right words to convey exactly how it feels for us, we become silent and almost embarrassed that we cannot say what we mean. What we do not realise is that not everything can be understood with words. The most delicate and powerful ideas and emotions are expressed in silence through the vibration of the individuals involved. People in love know this. Manipulators do too.

Have you ever been in front of someone you have never met before and made a deep connection with that person without needing any words? Have you connected the same way with a passer by? Have you been stopped in the street by someone coming in the opposite direction who has asked you to blow in his eye? Have you been lost in town and approached someone in a parked car to ask the way and as they looked at you, before speaking, the connection was so powerful you could hardly stand on your feet? Have you been in different shops where the attendants or owners knew exactly what you wanted down to the minutest details, without words?

If we become observers, we will clearly hear how so many people speak and use more words than are necessary. Often they repeat themselves to the point of being boring or irritating. Some speak without knowing what they are saying. They do it out of habit or to break the silence. It can be that as ideas come into their heads, they have to let them out. It can be amusing for a while but certainly tiring for a prolonged time.

Too many words change a situation from bad to worse because, in wanting to improve it, more words are used, to the point that there is no control of what is said and the wrong word drops in with a tremendous impact. Also, talking about a problem over and over again can make it bigger and more difficult to deal with.

Fewer words can save delicate situations and find solutions to what was thought to be a problem. Often, keeping silent is even better. After events have evolved, one is aware of how wise it was to choose one's words.

There are times when we love to hear the sounds of beautiful words in prose, poetry or even coming from individuals with warm and kind voices, which soothe us into relaxation and wellbeing.

We love to hear words of wisdom and love, and are grateful for them.

RUNNING AGAINST TIME

We live in a hectic society where everyone seems to be running to get somewhere or do something. When talking to people, the first thing that comes up is that they do not have enough time or that their diary is full.

When we feel the need to reach certain targets or overbook ourselves with things we think need doing, we create an inner rush in ourselves that can lead to stress, which in turn can lead to something else. It will happen without us being aware until our physical body manifests it in one way or another. We become obsessed with the thing to do rather than how we feel doing it. For example, we have to do something by a certain time and it is not happening because there have been interferences we could not avoid. Now we are late. We will not meet our targets or do what we had programmed to do. Our physical body feels discomfort and is ill at ease. We become preoccupied and stressed, as we rush towards our goal.

In these situations, we forget completely the importance of who we are and what is good and beneficial to us. We are running against our notion of time. That sense of time we have makes us behave in an unnecessary manner. First of all, we have that burning inner sensation of running against time, knowing well that we cannot catch time, because it does not exist. However, we do not stop the race to ponder over that, we carry on running. Many of us have had that feeling of heat going through our body when we missed a plane, train or bus, or when we missed an important meeting or conference because of traffic or delays in public transport. That feeling also comes just before getting to an appointment, conference or any other thing. The fact of wanting to run against time is there, making us feel beyond ourselves, and yet we do not consider stopping and listening to our body, taking on board how it feels, assessing it and dealing with it.

Our focus is only on what we missed. Disappointment makes us feel a strange vacuum inside. From that point reactions will vary according to each individual. By changing the scenario and not following the notion of going after time, we accept the fact that what has happened has happened, and we move forward into our new now. Then our true Self will take us smoothly through whatever is ahead of us and everything will end well. Often the results will surpass those we had initially expected by a long way.

Awareness of how we feel will keep us sensitive to the signs the body gives us. We hear people saying they have a headache, stomach-ache or are not feeling well and we see them carrying on without paying attention to the alarm the body is signalling them. It would be so much easier to stop and find out why the body is throwing that signal at them. Then they could deal with it and put an end to the discomfort.

Have you noticed that when you set your mind on arriving somewhere on time, you will do so no matter what the odds may be? On the other hand, have you noticed that when you feel nervous because you are afraid of arriving late, all kinds of things will happen and you will be late? In these cases it is common, if driving, to catch all the red lights on the way, more traffic than usual or anything else that will hinder our arrival on time.

Awareness of our now makes us timeless and therefore exempt from worries about time. When we are aware, we can live a life filled with joy and peace and the whole world will benefit from it.

DETACHMENT

· ·

Detachment is essential for moving forward. When we are attached, no matter to what or to whom, we are somehow held back. Detachment gives us freedom and makes us at peace with ourselves.

Being emotionally attached is a burden, no matter what the emotion may be. It keeps us from using our full potential. It is the break that stops us from being what we are because we stop to consider what is around us, and that could hinder our moves in any direction we may wish to take. By that we do not mean to be emotionless, but to be our true selves and respond to our inner inclination.

Detachment is extensive and we can find ourselves lost in its many avenues and criteria that can give way to misinterpretations. We can see this in close relationships. When discussing the subject, one of the partners may say that detachment is the best way to carry on with the relationship. If the full meaning of the word "detachment" is not understood there will be problems, and the one who does not understand it will treat the word as "abandonment", "separation", "indifference" or anything but the right meaning.

When we work on our self-development, detachment plays a big part because we have the freedom to move without anyone or anything pulling us back.

We hear people say that they cannot make a trip they would very much like to because their partners do not like travelling. Imagine being trapped because your spouse is holding you back emotionally. There are all kinds of examples where people are emotionally attached and that cord keeps them from being themselves and doing what they most like doing.

When we are detached from our husbands or wives, parents or children, friends, homes or objects, we are closer to them. Our love and dedication is stronger: it comes from the natural source rather than from our impermanent feelings that keep changing according to our moods and the influences that move them. Loving with detachment is a more reliable love, more sincere and honest. It is transparent, free from envy, jealousy, manipulation, guilt and more. It gives us peace of mind, a sense of belonging to the whole world and the whole world belonging to us in equal terms. There are those who will find this idea far-fetched, because they tend to be sceptical about anything new coming their way. Being open to the new will encourage our expansion and creativity.

If you are very tightly attached, it may be painful to pull away and it can take time. But the same pain that hurts you when you are becoming detached is the pain that kept hurting you when you were attached. The difference is that attachment equals pain and detachment equals freedom and wellbeing.

You may feel you are detached when you speak with your intellect. If you go to your emotions you may feel different. When you detach yourself from whatever or whomever you choose to, you will feel the difference. It is like jumping from discomfort to comfort and there is a sensation of relief as if you have dropped a heavy weight you were carrying for no purpose other than to create turmoil in your life.

When we are free, we are empowered. When we are attached, we move according to the cords that are pulling us from place to place without our being aware. Awareness is the key to being free.

HIDDEN POCKETS

. . . .

I t is amazing how some people have the ability to find pockets in which to store emotions, unpleasant situations and painful memories - anything that is hurtful in their lives. By observing it, we came to the conclusion that it could be a kind of mechanism that protects them from falling apart and ceasing to function in society.

Children are very good at this. When there is a crisis in the family, which could be illness, financial problems or separation of the parents, most children appear to cope well. They do not exteriorise how they feel or talk about it. One hears parents and relatives commenting on how well the children are coping with the situation, whatever the situation is.

Adults have different ways of doing this. Some will do what children do. Others will pretend nothing is happening, saying for example: "My wife (or husband) left me, but I have put that behind me already. It has gone from my mind". Has it really? Did they not find a pocket to store it in? Where? They may not know. However, it is pocketed somewhere, waiting for the right moment to come out in an illness, depression or any other symptom. There are those who will use alcohol or drugs to drown themselves into oblivion. There are also those who run away from the problems facing them and do not stop running because wherever they go the problems follow them. They do not realise that the problem is inside them and not in the places they go to or the people they meet. There are also those who blame everything that happens to them on other people. It could be their family, their job and colleagues. They think only they know how to do things and that everyone else is abusing the wellbeing of society. The list could go on.

There are the ones who suffer verbal diarrhoea when putting down anything and everything they choose in order to put themselves in the right place. Their words are real pollution, charged with damaging energy for us all. These people need help. It is important for all of us that they get help so that they stop putting out negative fuel into the atmosphere.

Everyone in crisis needs help, some more than others. Some are too proud to accept help because they think they can cope. Or they can even go into denial about what is happening to them. Caution is recommended when approaching those in suffering, because we do not know how affected they may be inside themselves. Appearances are deceiving and can fool anyone.

One thing is clear: those pockets have to be emptied. But how? There are many ways in which it can be done, depending on the situation or individual. If they do not know how to do it themselves, the best way is to ask for help. And again, the help available is as diverse as the people in need of it. The important thing is to make a start, no matter where one is, and keep going.

Being in silence, listening to your heart, take on board what you hear or sense: that would be the best start for everyone. No one is the same and even if issues look so similar, we are all so different in our own ways. Remember that we can be guided to all the knowledge and all the help we may need via our own heart, when we listen to it attentively and in silence. Meditation will help to calm the mind. There are many ways you can meditate. We can all learn. The possibilities are infinite. We can all make a difference to our society and to the world by having a clear mind and a loving heart.

WHEN WE COMPARE OUR CAPACITY TO THAT OF OTHERS

The results of comparing are not exact or real, not valid in any circumstances when they are used to compare the capacity of human beings or indeed any natural species.

Many people have idols. For some these can be in the world of sport, arts and entertainment. For others, they can be in the world of politics, finances and law. It can be anyone: a parent, brother, sister, friend or teacher. The chosen person is placed on a pedestal, out of reach of the person who puts this chosen one there. By thinking so highly of the admired person, you create a distance between the two of you. One is above and the other is below. The one below wishes to be like the one above but thinks himself unable to reach so high. It is an unconscious and general feeling. There are always exceptions.

Imagine you are a good singer and, with all your merits, you have a singing idol, whom you adore. You would never compare yourself to your idol without thinking that your idol is above you. You always consider your idol above yourself and even though you think you are a good singer, you are going to see yourself below your idol. This is what happens when you idolise someone, no matter in what field and for what reasons.

It is like having a dream and you stop it from coming true by putting someone in front of you, blocking the passage for you to go through the same door as that person you idealise or think is better than you. Here you are not allowing your true Self to come through and manifest your great capacity in whatever field the comparison takes place. It is important to value your skills and how able you are. There is no need to compare. If you can appreciate whatever each one of you can produce, you will enjoy the product offered by both of you without comparisons.

Some people, particularly the very able, frequently neglect their self-esteem. Often they are unaware of this, unless it is brought to their attention by an incident or someone pointing it out to them. It is wise to keep self-esteem high. Whether someone has low or high self-esteem, it is very noticeable from their behaviour and the way they speak.

When you are yourself and allow yourself to be your true Self, you are always in the right place. It would not occur to you that someone is better than you or not. You just are as you are. You have different roles to play. You came with different programmes, even though you may be in the same family, business or way of life. You still have different programmes and roles to play and no matter how similar they are, they are unique to you and no one else could take your place or you anyone else's. You can always become better at whatever you do. The possibilities are infinite. Time and space are given to you to expand according to your specific role in the game you are playing, which is the game of life. The rules of the game can change as and when you want. Who you play with can also vary according to your wishes, which are directed by your thoughts. As your thoughts are moving constantly, so is everything else. The whole of our physical experience is in constant movement and change. The clue is to be in harmony with who you are and true to your true Self in order to vibrate in unison with your most wanted desires. You are a precious piece of the whole as is everyone. Being aware of this brings us to the present moment.

ACCEPTANCE

There are different types of acceptance. The type we hear most about is that of accepting things in life in a passive way, which does not serve us. We accept the inevitable such as where we were born, being short or tall, or having good looks or not, because there is not much we can do about them, although in today's world our looks can be modified.

Let us concentrate on the type of acceptance we may find difficult and we struggle with. We position ourselves at a certain level and from there we have our expectations. We expect to meet the right person to marry and we think we have done that, at least until after some years when the routines take over. By then we have another picture of the person we chose to share our life with. Of course, we do not take into account the fact that we all change constantly and, without realising it, we may branch out in opposite directions, which will bring obstacles into the relationship. Then the children arrive, needing a lot of our time. This is a sensitive time for any relationship and brings great responsibilities. Acceptance starts to play an important role as hidden characteristics of the couple come to light, which we may like to accept or reject. Another element of the game is in play.

When we look at acceptance, we only do so from the small mind, which can only see the physical world, from a short term perspective. That leaves a big gap, which a minority are happy to access. Then they find out that there is more to life than what they thought. They find there is a well of information within that supposedly empty gap. It is within us and anyone has access to it. You only need the desire to find it. When we access it, we find there are certain things in our lives that we have not liked for a long time and we have accepted living with them. They were obstacles put in our way for us to learn certain lessons, which we would otherwise not have had the opportunity to learn. Tricky situations are often put in our way so we learn to deal with them and change them accordingly. It is for us to know whether the situations should be changed or accepted, and act upon them as we best know how. If we miss this opportunity, we will be given other opportunities.

Accepting the fact that we are as we are, and especially being true to our true Self, is the most important thing we need to know.

We may find it hard to accept when we see family, friends or the world in pain. But that is one of our lessons here on earth. We find it hard to accept certain behaviour due to a particular condition in our loved ones, and it is harder still to live with it day by day. However, when we come to know that it is all right to be as we have chosen to be, then accepting it becomes easier. When we understand that the situations of that behaviour are there partly to help us with our own learning and experiencing life in as many ways as possible, then we happily accept it. This acceptance is the most beautiful because it comes from knowing who we are and being aware of our temporary time on earth, for we know that where we came from we are all perfect in every way. So, there is no need to feel sorrow or envy at others' gifts. We know their gifts are ours as well, but they are not to be displayed by us this time around. Accepting that which makes us perfect in whatever imperfection we may find ourselves and knowing the condition is there for a particular purpose will give us freedom and peace. We will feel gratefulness, for the harder the lesson the greater the reward.

SERENITY AND INNER TRUST THAT ALL IS WELL

You may wonder how anyone can be serene in a world of turmoil? We would say it is in our nature to be serene. We do not have to find a state of being, because it is our most precious possession, together with Universal Love and intelligence.

People are astonished to hear children come up with brilliant insights, or see young people being great achievers. There are heroes, geniuses and very talented individuals. Often these special people started their lives in a world of much turmoil for them. They had nothing and yet they pushed up to the very top, where they are known for their strength and power for reaching such heights, coming from precarious and difficult beginnings. What do they have that the rest of humanity does not have?

They have serenity in themselves, in the inner core of themselves and they trust it. For they know they may live in a world of turmoil, but that what counts is the kind of world within themselves. They know all will be well if they trust in themselves and put to use the many gifts they were given before setting out on this journey. They believe in what they have within and allow it to work. They communicate with their inner world and allow it to guide them through whatever may come their way. They know well that the important thing is not the exterior world and how it may seem to be, but their interior world where they find themselves face to face with themselves. There they see who they are and what they can do. Reaching this point is vital for keeping serene in spite of all the odds.

One thing to remember is that we all have the same possibilities and are given the same gifts. The thing is to realise that important fact. Have you noticed how difficult it is to be kind to yourself? Even some who are well established in their professions doubt if they are good enough.

There are no secrets about being in the right place at the right time so that life smiles on us the way we wish. There are as many different smiles as there are lives. That is how it is supposed to be, but it is not important because we know we can change it should we want to.

Serenity is not being gained because it exists in us already. If we have not found it, it is because we have not been aware of it, even though it is within us. Trust is knowing who we are. Once we know who we are everything becomes clear and smooth, in other words serene.

Silence in the mind, meditation, time spent with ourselves, reflecting on our impact on others and society at large, all help to put us in the right place to reach our maximum achievement for ourselves and the world. We do well to remember that by hurting others we hurt ourselves. Loving others, we love ourselves. Whether we believe this or not is not going to change the nature of things and how the Supreme Universal Intelligence has given us all the tools to work out how to reach our goals. One of them is to love and help the world we live in, starting by loving and helping ourselves.

Thus serenity and trust will be our best friends.

STOPPING DOING THINGS

People can be running from one place to another, doing one thing or another, and there is exhaustion in their comings and goings. It is like pursuing the unattainable: it produces tiredness and, for some, anxiety and fatigue.

When we stop completely, regardless of what may remain for us to do, we will find a sensation of relief as if the world has suddenly stopped for us. For a while, we do not know what to do or how to fit into that time-slot. Gradually we adjust to the stillness, and then the mind calms down too. Going on retreats helps and if they are silent retreats it helps still more. They are holistic boosters. Being away from our daily routines and forgetting about the notion that we have so much to do or not to do can be of extraordinary help. To stop is to recharge our system, allowing it to rest and sink back into balance and wellbeing.

Stopping doing things is not a holiday. Holidays can be hectic. Experience will tell us that going on holidays is doing things to the maximum, because maybe this is the only time we have to experience the surroundings or activities we normally do not have time for. On the other hand, some people will rest, read and go for walks. Even the fact of choosing a book or a walk requires decision-making. What we want is to stop completely and do what comes to us remotely and effortlessly whether we need to do it or not.

We may think that the mind does not need rest. We reassure ourselves by resting the body, believing that if we have a rested body we are not tired. When the mind is active for hours on end and does not give productive results, and when it turns in circles around unsolved issues, that can be the most exhausting thing we can experience.

By being in silence, we are allowing our higher Self to come forward and there will be communication with our body and mind. By listening attentively, a flow of information will be coming through that allows us to be our real selves and perform at a rate of Excellence.

Stopping the mind for seconds is really good. Stopping it for minutes is excellent. Stopping it for hours is a blessing.

IGNORING BASIC INFORMATION

Through information and knowledge we find out who we are and our mission on the planet. It is most important for us to be able and free to do this. As children, we may be directed to do what we do not want to do. That could be taking us away from what we came to do and it could mess things up for many of us. However, circumstances can be part of our challenges designed by us.

The states of the planet and its frequencies have a lot to do with how we are going to find our lives on it. The choices we made when choosing our parents and the countries we were going to live in matter too. When we arrive on earth we are well prepared with information regarding the planet and the people on it. We know everything there is to know for us to have a successful journey, with the exception that we arrive in a physical body which is weighed down by heavy energies as opposed to the ones we are used to before coming. This body gives us trouble in many ways. We cannot manage by ourselves. It takes a long time for us to adjust to the way of life here. We depend on others. We are trained to do as they do. That is very hard. Adults cannot see what children see. Children are ahead of them in everything. However, through the disciplines imposed on children by the society they have chosen to live in, after a few years they forget what they came to do. This tends to coincide with the age they start school.

What seems to have happened in the past, with the exception of a small minority, is that children were forced to follow whatever the parents or community were doing, regardless of the special gifts they came with. Adults believe that they are superior in knowledge to their children and that is not the case. Fortunately, in television programmes looking for talent in kids we can discover the genius in them that otherwise would have been repressed or ignored. We see 18 month old babies speaking and counting, 3 year olds knowing the capitals of the countries of the whole world. When given the country they will say its capital straight away without hesitation. From babies up to the age of seven an amazing number of children in every country reveal what they know and adults are taken aback by this phenomenon. A five-year-old girl can sing like a soprano or a boy the same age like a tenor. The examples are infinite. Thanks to the digital world we live in, we can see all this from our own home. Generally speaking, most people will be surprised and in disbelief of such things. We wonder how many go deeper than that. How many of us can say, "Hold on a moment, why is this happening? Is there something we do not know? How can we find out?" This lack of interest keeps most people in ignorance of basic and important knowledge.

We have to remember that our best teachers are our children, if we listen to them and allow them to be their true selves. Every time we repress a child we lose a genius. Some of them will rediscover themselves later in life when they can survive without adult care. This ignorance on the part of adults has unwanted results for us all. When people do not know, they create their own version of situations that have not taken place yet. They feel fear and pain from them as if they were already living those situations. Unfortunately, they ignore that the stories they imagine and feel so strongly are created by them thinking and vibrating in that way. They think that worrying is normal, when it is not. They think that suffering for people who are ill or dying is normal, but it is not normal. Our true Self does not accept those feelings and thoughts as our own, because they are not. We are beyond that limitation. We are not our physical body. Our ignorance leads us to attach too much importance to the physical world, including our body. We are limitless.

THINGS ARE GETTING BETTER

Whether we are aware of it or not, things are getting better all the time, unless we block the process and the flow by not allowing it. Expansion is moving constantly in unison with movement and change. Changes are not always what we want to have and the contrary happens too. Nevertheless, changes continue to be with us and evolution moves on.

Day to day we hardly notice those changes we are familiar with. Mothers will realise that clothes are getting small on their children and this sometimes comes as a surprise to them. The children have grown. As we get to a certain age, no matter how active we are and how well we feel, we will be surprised by how long it takes us to do something we could do before in the blink of an eye. All things around us change as we do.

We change the place where we live, the jobs we do, the partners we live with, the way we dress, the way we eat and what we eat. We change opinions incessantly and our tastes for things and people. We change our moods and behaviour. In short, everything is changing. People worry when the nation changes government, finances go up or down, worldwide disasters happen. They rejoice when science advances and humans can do astonishing things they could not do before.

One thing that is still hard to accept for many people is when they lose a loved one. Death means the end of everything for them. "Passed away" and "passed on" seem more like transcending into other levels of existence. This change in the termination of our programme on earth, going back to where we came from, to what we really are, causes much suffering amongst almost everyone except those who live close to their true selves. The latter know that dropping our physical body does not mean we die and disappear forever. No, it means we have finished what we came to do here on earth. We could not possibly survive on this planet without a physical body. So the universe gives us that facility, which we use the best way we can. Our suffering comes when we forget this truth. When the masses forget this outcome it is worse for all of us. Awakening to this truth is the way to help us and the world.

Any change, no matter what it is, is a step forward in evolution and expansion. We accept some changes with joy and others with pain. This is because some favour our senses and others do not. In order for expansion to take place at all levels there have to be contrasts. The contrasts can be acceptable to us provided they do not interfere with the comforts and routines of our lives. However, if changes take us into the unknown, we have a tendency to be against them, resisting them to the point of harming ourselves without realising it. We can find the unknown daunting.

One thing is good for sure: no matter what changes occur in our lives, things are always getting better. We may not be aware of this, but it is when the years have gone by and we look back that we realise how certain changes we were afraid of have improved our life. This does not refer to material wealth, but rather the round of knowledge and experiences lived through.

Things are always getting better and changes help the process. Wakening to this fact will save time and energy. It will keep us younger and happier because we know how to proceed on our way.

WE ARE LEARNING

The potential of learning is within us permanently. We learn as we live. We keep learning and relearning what we already know and have forgotten. As we move in different time lines, we have varied experiences of existence from which we keep learning again and again, always with the objective of expanding more and more and ascending higher and higher.

Some people have an insatiable thirst for learning, regardless of their social rank or job. We have the privilege these days of learning anything we want from our own home. That is so important for the learner, whether they be a simple gardener or a big agricultural producer. Learning differs from one job or profession to another and advances according to how the people involved in them learn. The procedure seems to be to start at the bottom and move up to higher positions according to the speed with which each individual learns.

The way we all learn and the access we have to learning differs according to our starting point. It is also affected by our interests or needs, whether we can afford to go to the schools we may wish to go to, the importance our parents may give to education, or the laws of the country regarding education for all, and so on.

Learning is driven by a thirst for wanting to know more, a sense of curiosity, and an inquisitive mind constantly asking the question "what if?" It is like an itch in the mind that keeps nagging. Those who follow that nagging achieve great things.

Learning injects interest and enthusiasm into life. Without it our lives are dull, lacking in sparkle or joy. "Live and learn", they say. Learning through experiencing life is a good way of understanding what we are learning. How many times have we thought we knew something until we experienced it? Then, we changed our mind on the subject. That taught us that one thing is to see it through the intellect and another is to experience it in life. The understanding is deep and the satisfaction profound.

We start learning from the moment we are born and never stop. Even those who do not want to learn still learn by default. They may say, "I've seen it all. I know it all. I've done it all. I'm not interested". They are stuck in a sequence, and by denying it they will be stuck until they ask for help to be released from it. There are many joyless places. There are many more joyful ones. Which would you choose to be in? You could be the one reaching out for a hand to pull you out into the light or you could be the one who hears the call for help and runs to give it. Where do you fit in?

Every morning when we get up, we are met by a new fresh day. Although days and places may look the same day after day, they are not because of the constant changes taking place. Therefore, we are stepping onto renewed ground all the time. The fact that we may reject this idea or accept it does not change a bit what it is, what it has been and what it will be.

A good practice would be to ask ourselves before we go to sleep each night how many things we have learned that day and ponder on how many more there are out there for us to learn still. Being aware makes our experience of learning more exciting and fulfilling.

EMPOWERMENT

. . . .

I t is extremely important for us to be empowered at all times, especially at this time of such huge planetary changes. Being empowered means we know who we are. We feel the energies for what they are and we distinguish their differences, even in the smallest objects.

What do we mean by being empowered? It means we stand in our reality. We know who we are and we know our power. We know we are powerful beings and radiate light because we are light. We do not need other people to come and tell us that, as used to be the case in the past when we needed saviours. No one is going to save us but ourselves. We are our own saviours. We pass on this information by word of mouth, without the need to follow anyone in particular. This is the time when we realise how powerful we all are, and by being together on the positive side of love and care we can make a great difference to ourselves and to the whole world.

People become disempowered when they give their power to someone else voluntarily, or when they consider themselves to be less than others in whatever situation. There are power predators who steal power from people and leave them feeling vulnerable and weak. When they are weak they can easily be manipulated and taken advantage of. This is why manipulators will use techniques to break people, making them feel they are nothing and worthless. Once their self-esteem is gone, these people are easy prey.

Those who want power for themselves will use a range of tools to achieve it. The most efficient tool is fear. Fear can be created on a national level or even on a worldwide level, so they can conquer the world.

We are universal beings who are experiencing life on planet earth. There are those who have forgotten their identity and how powerful they are. So it is time for an awakening to take place so we realise how wonderful and able we all are, how powerful we all are. Each one of us can manage our power. We no longer need helpers. In fact some of us have known this for a long time, and now the moment has come for everyone to take responsibility for themselves. Being empowered gives us choices.

It becomes extremely important to be aware of what we think, what we feel and what we do. Words carry power and make strong impacts on others, and at a universal level too. It is good to remember the Law of Attraction: what we vibrate we will attract. Paying attention to our thoughts and our words at all times will help us be in a position of using words to benefit ourselves and the whole. If we do not have anything pleasant to say, it is better not to say anything at all. Making sure the questions we ask have a definite purpose will bring us the right answers, rather than asking questions to break the silence. The same thing would apply to comments we make. Being alert, aware and mindful of our thoughts will be a way we can make a difference.

How do we know we are empowered? We are empowered when we know who we are, when our self-esteem is high, when we know we are LOVE and we love ourselves like no one else can, when we know how to communicate with our true Self, when we know all other humans have the same power as us. No one is below or above us. We all have access to the same source of power. It is up to us to recognise it.

FRIENDS -1 -

. . . .

What do we mean by friends? Friends can be seen in various ways and colours. They can have depth or they can be superficial. They can be faithful or they can betray us. They can be helpful or selfish. They can be kind or abusive. In fact, friends can fit all the descriptions of humans.

Most of us have had good and bad experiences with those we thought were our friends. Have you noticed that as soon as we give someone the title of "friend", this person becomes a part of our life and therefore of inevitable expectations? More often than not, expectations bring disappointments that we neglect to prepare ourselves for.

We engage in friendships without noticing the masks they are wearing when they are with us. We are exposing ourselves to many things. Some are very good at making us believe what they are not. By contrast, there are those who come to us with a clear and loving heart. It is up to us to distinguish which vibrations match ours in the best way possible in order to build a friendly relationship. Due to the diversity of human interests, personalities and characters, when it comes to making real friends who will last the trials of life, it is important to allow the universe to choose for us.

Life usually does a great job for us placing friends in different categories. There are those we can trust, those we connect with, those we have fun with, those with good contacts, those we can call on and so forth. These so-called friends may cease to be friends when life casts a light on them and we can see through them. Then we know we are not suited but we can carry on being distant friends. It may pay off to be aware of the friends who use or abuse us. Sometimes best friends do the worst things to us. Other times, our expectations of our friends are so high that they cannot meet them. The friends we feel at home with are those we trust. They are solid and always there for us, no matter what the occasion. If those we connect with fall into the category of trustworthy as well they become blessings in our lives.

When friends let us down in a bad way, they mark our lives with sadness. The impotence we feel is overwhelming, mainly because we do not understand how such great friendship has been treated with lightness and indifference. We are not prepared to let go. We are not ready for that big change in our lives. We thought it would last forever, but did not bear in mind that changes come along to make us grow in different ways through different routes for our benefit and wellbeing. Instead of being sad, we will do better being grateful for the good times we had together and the many things we learned in each other's company. Awareness tells us when the job is done. Then it is time to move on.

The main thing for us is to focus on being as sincere, trustworthy, kind, helpful, knowledgeable, wise, interesting and amusing as the friends we want to find, so that our vibrations will match those we are looking for and we will attract them into our lives.

We have to bear in mind that we cannot expect others to be full of good qualities without examining those we have ourselves. That does not mean we have to have exactly the same qualities. But they may complement or enhance those the other person has. The point is, not to take for granted what our friends to be may bring to us, and to pay attention to what we have to offer to make a good match and hopefully a lasting one, providing we allow space for changes and opportunities, which can take us into multiple experiences but not always together.

FRIENDS - 2 -

"Friend" is the label we give to people who are close to us because of interests we may have in common or through work. We enjoy their company and have fun with them. Life gives us many opportunities to find friends.

Somehow as we make friends they fall into an appropriate category by themselves without us categorising them. Have you noticed how, according to our mood or what we want, we know who to call to spend time with us or join us for a particular activity? Without any judgement and according to the activity we will be doing, the names of those we want to be with will immediately come into our mind, because we know they will enjoy what we want to do.

There are those who find it difficult to make friends. They may be shy. They possibly lack self-esteem. Lacking self-esteem puts people on a step lower than everyone else. It is as if they cannot reach the step others are on, and therein lies the difficulty of making friends. There is a resistance in them and usually they are not aware of it, but when they are accepted, they open up and show their amazing skills. On the other hand, there are those who make friends very easily. They are open to whoever they meet. Some will become friends and others acquaintances. It does not mean that their self-esteem is high, but their openness allows them to relate well. They have a good innate skill. There are many varieties of friendship, according to our tendencies and ways of life.

If we are lucky to have good friends who we can understand and trust, we know the blessing of having friends there for us at all times. However, it can happen that we believe in those friends, but when we need them and call on them, they are like empty vessels: they have nothing to offer or are unwilling to offer anything. It is a painful situation. There is one useful thing to bear in mind: these situations are given to us in order to fulfil our project on our journey. On the other hand, we meet people who we love and become quite attached to, yet our lives take different routes unknown to us. We are meant to encounter everyone we meet on our path so we can finish something unfinished or learn something new.

Soul friends are rare and yet we meet them. Sometimes it can be as briefly as minutes or it can last for months or years, and there may be those who last a lifetime. These are the lucky ones. Soul friends experience the depth of both their souls meeting and melting into one with no need for words because they are one. Whatever one thinks, the other is thinking it at the same time. Imagine the harmony between those souls. These experiences are unforgettable. They may feel similar to when two people fall in love, but it is not the same. It is a higher and purer feeling. It is a taste of freedom in the sense that we are all one. That goes beyond what words can explain.

On our journey we may realise that our true Self is our best friend. When we realise this truth, we become content. We can rely on the fact that our true Self is always with us and never leaves us. It can give us anything we ask for and assist us every second of our life. We are grateful to have it in us.

BEING GRATEFUL

· ·

How often a day do we say "thank you" for the many things in front of our eyes every second? How often do we thank those behind the scenes who work for us to be able to live the way we do and enjoy the comforts we have? How often do we look around us dazzled and, in gratitude, give thanks for what we see? How often do we thank those around us for being part of our experience on earth? How often do we thank ourselves for just being us?

We do not need to spend additional time being grateful and saying "thank you". We can be grateful as we walk along or do our job or housework. We can show gratefulness in many ways: with a smile, a gesture, a look, a gentle touch, putting our hand to our heart, with words and caring how we use them, with our thoughts and intentions, with a flower or small detail and with a combination of them all.

When we feel grateful, we feel empowered and connected to Source. We all deserve to have all those things which make us feel good about the world and ourselves.

We can easily give thanks for the good things in life and forget to thank what we think of as bad things because they may bring pain or sadness. However, those are very often what lead us into happiness and fulfilment. The contrasts make us appreciate more what is on the other side. Seeing ungratefulness in someone's face is painful; seeing gratefulness is joyful. Depending how the gratefulness is expressed, it can be emotional and touch us deeply. Being in a state of gratefulness elevates us, and we may feel as if our feet do not touch the ground because our sensations are so light. This happens to some of us when we are in nature amongst its beauty and amazing displays or art. It feels good thanking the Creator at the beginning of each day for allowing us to be in it and at the end of the day for all the things that made it possible for us to achieve our goals.

Being grateful is a state of being. It is when we appreciate everything and everyone, including ourselves - very especially ourselves. It is when we are in awe at everything that happens around us and feel privileged to experience it. It is when we see kindness in the eyes of people and innocence in the eyes of children. It is when we see the skilful performances of the collective that make us want to thank the whole. It is when we do not take anything or anyone for granted and realise the importance of everything that occurs on our journey. It may be difficult to be grateful to those who do their best to be in our way and obstruct our path; but they are doing it for our sake so that we will be able to remove hidden energies which otherwise we would not be aware of. So what may seem to be an annoyance is a blessing in disguise for us. Those who create that situation do not know why they are doing it. Bearing this in mind, it is important for us to be grateful rather than unpleasant to those whose job is to make others aware of their burdens which need to be released. Once the energies blocking us have gone, we feel lighter and grateful for it.

Love and gratefulness go hand in hand. When we feel deeply grateful we feel love towards the object of our gratitude. When our giving and receiving is sincere, we can feel it running through our whole body. Being aware of these feelings brings us closer to our true Self. We experience its delicious and beautiful sensations.

BEING FOCUSED

· ·

Being focused is so important in life. When we are focused we can concentrate one hundred per cent on what we do and the results are brilliant. We save time and resources, and especially energy. We get to the point, flow smoothly, and enjoy whatever we are involved in. Distractions can get in the way and make us weaker or stronger. It depends on us.

In a world of so many distractions, it takes perseverance and discipline to retain our attention and be focused for long periods of time. There are exceptions: when people love to do something with passion, their attention is always on that particular thing and it is hard to lose focus. It works for them. However, those who do that may neglect other necessary and important aspects of their life.

From the moment we are born, those around us start asking us to focus on something or other. When we go to school it becomes harder. Most children would prefer to be playing than focusing on a history lesson for instance. Their minds wander all over the place, to the point that they forget they are in class and they stop hearing what is going on. As adults the same thing happens. Have you been in meetings when your mind wanders on to other things rather than listening to the speaker, or the discussion that may be going on? Have you been doing your job and your mind takes you somewhere else? Then, mistakes happen. We often hear expressions such as: "I don't know what I was thinking", "my mind just went and I forgot about it", "I got distracted by…", "Oh! What was I thinking about?" The mind wanders unless we learn how to keep it in the present moment. There are techniques that can help us to be focused.

It is easy to be focused at all times when we are in our centre. Being in our centre gives us the flexibility of moving with changes that may occur around us. Otherwise we would not notice. Being in our centre is like being guided by our Satellite Navigation. It tells us where to go and which road would be more suitable to take.

We attract what our mind is on. So it is in our interest to keep it on those things we want to manifest in our life. An unfocused mind goes all over the place, and then we encounter distortions in our way. We may moan and complain about them and that will bring more of the same. Many people fall into cycles created that way. This happens because of lack of information or knowledge. To get out of these cycles we ask for help if we cannot find it in ourselves.

It is MOST IMPORTANT TO KNOW that we have within us everything we may be looking for outside ourselves. We are that powerful. Of course, if we do not have this knowledge or information it is wise to find ways of acquiring it. One thing to remember is that however we may find information we transform it into what suits us individually. No matter how much sameness we have with others, we are still individually different in some aspects of our life. Focusing on who we really are, focusing on our true Self and being with it all the way, we are safe and can reach the most amazing goal of our life on earth. A lot of people do that and many more are joining in. We can all do it. When we do it we become examples for others to learn from, and it will be good to show them that their path is different and they have to focus on their individual way. It is like teaching a child how to ride a bicycle: once they are on it and moving, they know what to do on their own. Keeping our individuality and knowing we have the power within us is essential.

TEACHING

We are all teachers, and we are all students at the same time. We are always teaching someone and we are always learning from someone.

When we take the role of being a teacher, no matter in what circumstances, patience is the quality that will bring success to both teacher and learner. With patience and love we learn best.

Teachers of all subjects we are talking to you. If you are a teacher by profession you are privileged to have so many people you can share what you know with. You will excel if you teach from the heart and without ego. Those who allow the ego to be present when they teach will hurt many vulnerable students and raise anger in others. They may know their subject well but lack skills to deliver it. So their teaching is damaging rather than useful.

There are also those teachers who know their subject, but passing it on becomes hindered by personal or family problems they carry with them: they lash its venom onto the students. They may go for one or more students, maybe the whole class. Any student who touches the weak area affected by their problems may be their target.

Teachers would be wise to be aware that the children they are teaching already know the subject. What has happened is that they have forgotten it and only need to remove layers of dust that may be in the way. When that is done with love, knowledge and understanding the results excel in every way.

Parents take the role of teachers from the moment we arrive on the planet. There are all kinds of parents and they teach accordingly. It should not worry anyone because children choose their parents and the family they are born into. It is part of our project in the physical world. The family we choose suits us for what we came to do.

We are all teachers: at work, at home, with friends, in the street with strangers and in many situations. Patience, kind words, warm smiles and unconditional love will do very well. Their impact will stay with the learners for all their lives.

The most fascinating teaching is self-teaching and self-learning. We teach ourselves and we learn from ourselves. The fascinating bit comes when we read in a book or hear someone saying in a seminar all the things we already know, because those things came to us years before and we have been using them ever since. Some of us, at the beginning, thought it was unfair: unfair because we knew it for a long time and then someone said they had discovered it, or something similar. We can hear our ego shouting "I knew that and I have been practising it for a long time". It can take us a long time to give in before we become aware that knowledge is there, and has always been there for anyone who wants to help himself or herself to it. We have to be thankful that we were able to acquire the knowledge ourselves. This gave us the advantage of getting it from Source, free from the opinions of intermediaries, and thus one hundred per cent genuine. We can find ourselves in situations where someone has recommended a seminar by some well-known personality, but when we attend we find we already know what they are teaching. This is not disappointing; it is actually rather satisfying to know that we already have that information and it must be true if other people are saying the same things. We have been well self-taught.

TALKING

. . . .

Are we aware that talking is more than just making noises or expressing how we feel? Are we aware of the impact and consequences of our words? Are we aware of the sounds we make and how they affect our immediate surroundings and the whole planet? Are we aware of the words we use and our intonation when we utter them? If not, we ought to pay attention to what words come to us, how we use them, and why.

We all talk too much without being aware. More than is necessary. We repeat the same things over and over, filling our minds with garbage and infecting those who are listening to us. The national or local news on the radio or television is an example. If there is a tragedy, they go on and on talking about it for days. As if that were not enough, they invite people into the studio to go through it in minute detail. Are they aware of the impact they are having at the collective level? Those who benefit from it know. How about those presenting the program? How about the listeners who swallow what is thrown at them and then pass it on, discussing it with others for long periods of time or until another item of news takes over? This news can create fear, anxiety and physical illness. If we observe how people use words discussing the news, how they get agitated, sad, anxious or frightened, and how they take it at a personal level, we will realise the great need there is for awareness.

When we talk too much we lose control of our words and we may say what we did not intend to say. We sometimes talk to kill a silence which can make us feel uncomfortable due to a lack of security in ourselves. We talk to evade subjects we do not want to address. The truth of the matter is that we talk too much. Those who are aware of their words and measure them according to precise situations are in a minority. This minority does not share the same awareness of the use of words, because their interests are based on both sides of the coin and therefore opposites, producing very different results. It is up to us all to find out on which side of the coin we want to be. Free from words from other people, we can hear our own words that come from within our hearts and guide us onto the path we want to be on. To reach this point we want to remove useless and repetitive words and conversations from our lives. We want to be free and in silence. The words we want to hear will resonate in our hearts with a sound of wellbeing free from fear, anxiety and sadness, free from the heaviness others weigh on us.

Our job is to work on ourselves and make sure that the words we use are adequate to express with precision what is in our mind, without judgement, without anger, without envy or any other feeling which could affect us or anyone else in a negative way.

Some people can appear to be silent but within themselves there can be the noisiest thunder. It is so loud that they can find themselves drowning in it. Others are silent and inoffensive for lack of knowing what to say. There are other types of silent people, but we leave those for you to find out about.

It would be wise for us to allow our inner guidance to choose the necessary words for us to have a wonderful life. However, that does not exempt us from our responsibilities of paying attention to our thoughts, feelings and actions. Following the directions from our heart and unconditional love will be a pleasurable journey.

HEALING -1-

. . . .

The planet can heal itself and all of us. It has a great abundance of herbs, trees, precious stones and all kinds of materials that heal us from ailments created by ourselves through our ignorance in thinking and behaving. There are very enlightened people on the planet who know all the resources there are for healing. This help is at hand but there are still many people who have no desire to look for it.

The majority of us need to heal from past traumas and wounds which were not taken care of when they happened. They have been hiding in pockets in our different bodies: physical, emotional and mental. When we feel affected by those hidden energies, most of us are unaware that those pockets exist. Traditional medicine plays a role here and most people feel relieved because of that help. The truth of the matter is that often we can help ourselves through our own energy and our knowledge of it. For centuries this method was forbidden and punished because of the greed of some. Fear forbade this knowledge to be available, so bringing it back is proving quite a task. There are and have been very dedicated groups and individuals working towards showing us how to be in the light and remove blockages of energy that can cause illnesses. Teachings about how to heal ourselves have progressed tremendously in recent years, and now they are available from professionals everywhere.

Healing fear from the past and learning how to deal with present-day fear that is thrown at us constantly is our major concern at this moment in time. Natural changes are taking place very fast, so it is vital that those who ignore the universal teachings wake up before it is too late.

All of us can heal others and ourselves. It is natural for us to do that if we allow it. Of course, we have to remove shadows from the past, traumas and wounds that are still reminding us that they exist and want to be attended to. Once we are free from the burden we bear, we will be renewed. We will feel different and we will see the games we play in our physical existence. Then we can be our real true selves and life becomes bliss.

It is good to bear in mind that we all have the capacity to heal ourselves. The challenge for us is to do it. Just being who we really are can dissolve anxieties and doubts about ourselves and the world. It is time to leave behind fears of all kinds. It is a simple job to dissolve all these dark energies into the powerful light that we carry within our hearts. If you have not found it yet, look for it. It is there within you. There is no need to look for it anywhere else.

It is also good to be aware at all times that by healing ourselves we are healing our surroundings and the whole world. By helping ourselves, we are helping everyone else too. In the same way when we move a finger our whole nervous system moves. When we think, feel and act, we are moving the network of the whole collective existence. This is a major reason why taking responsibility for our life and how we live it is most important for the wellbeing of the whole.

HEALING - 2 -

• •

There are so many ways of healing these days that those who do not know what they want find it hard to choose from such a great variety of practitioners. Nature is and always has been at our disposal for healing by providing us with all we need around us.

More and more people realise that natural ways of healing are better for our health, since modern medicine can often only deal with the symptoms and does not heal the root of the problem. We now have experts on herbs telling us that just through infusions from a particular medicinal plant, tree or flower, we can heal ourselves from practically anything. There are thousands of plants that can heal us. We are so lucky to have the internet to find out which plant will be suitable for whatever condition. We can often grow these plants ourselves. The irony of it is that the pharmaceutical companies use the same plants, making them into tablets, syrups, powder or injections. The plants have gone from being natural to being made unnatural. It is in our interest to check what medicines we take and be aware of the consequences of what we may ingest.

We also have the many precious stones as well as ordinary rocks and pebbles from the beach, all of them offering us healing for different ailments. All stones have healing powers. The experts can also tell us which is the most appropriate for whatever we are suffering from and how to use it for best results. During a trip to South Africa, we were told we could use them for infusions too. We do not boil them as we do plants; we let the stone rest in water for an appropriate length of time.

All the elements are healers. In some countries, doctors send their patients to thermal spas. It seems to work for a lot of things, especially for rheumatism. Have you had a hot bath with sea salt and natural extract oils from plants or flowers in it? Have you soaked in it for at least half an hour? Tiredness, stress, heaviness and bad temper dissolve in it. We recover our good temper, strength and calmness. When feeling low or depressed, have you had the chance to walk by the sea? Go up a mountain? Walk amongst trees or just be in nature? Have you walked in the rain, allowing the water to soak you through? And have you been grateful for it? A lot of healing occurs with those simple actions. Awareness is the key.

Some people walk on hot coals. Those who do it never forget the experience because of the clearing of the negative energies they leave behind. That is real healing. Have you been in the countryside at night by a huge fire and your friends have challenged you to jump over it? You hesitated out of fear, but finally you jumped. Can you remember the sensation of wellbeing that stayed with you afterwards? That is healing.

Have you been outdoors and been bitten by a wasp or other insect, and then by putting mud on the bite the pain has gone? Some spas cover people with mud to relax them and make them feel better.

The air we breathe is the most powerful healer because it sustains our life in the physical world. When we pay attention to our breath, it takes us to the present moment. Being in the present moment means we are connected to Source and therefore feeling our true Self.

In different parts of the world they use these elements and the whole of nature in the most skilful ways to heal people. We are lucky to live in a world that allows us to use all those methods for our wellbeing.

There are lots of healing experts we can go to. They can guide us to a point, but they are not healing us. We are the healers. We heal ourselves. The power is in us. Without our will no healing takes place.

We can heal others with their permission or with Divine permission. We can do it in many ways with different techniques. These techniques work if the patient is with us or elsewhere in the world. The latter is what we call "distant healing". It works in the same way.

We were approached to heal a woman in her late 50s, whom we did not know and we had never met. She lived on the other side of the planet from where we lived. She had been ill for a long time and had seen many specialists and had been on innumerable drugs. But she was getting worse all the time. The doctors had told her that they could not do anything else. She was very worried and her family was too. We were approached by an intermediary and asked for distant healing. We gave instructions what to do. On the first day, we could not work with the patient. She was frightened of this new idea of healing and did not trust it. So she did not accept it. We could not do anything at all. We communicated with the intermediary by phone and explained the situation. The next day, the patient opened up and allowed us to work with her. Two days later we received news that she was getting better by the day. Within two weeks she had recovered completely.

We are so connected to each other that we can, with permission, manage that the energies in others be restored to health. However, the point we want to make is that we can do it ourselves. We all have that power. First, we have to believe it. Then, we can learn how to do it if need be. For so many of us, it is natural to be that way. This is why it is important to release all the fears we have and our lack of trust in ourselves, for these block our natural way of seeing what is inside us.

Let us remember at all times that we can change anything we wish when the work is done by our true Self; and for that we must be connected. Separations bring us stresses and illnesses. As for being connected, it brings alignment to the power within that can heal us in every way we wish through the power of thought. As always, the choice is ours.

KNOWLEDGE

. . . .

Knowledge is the biggest treasure we can acquire and, whether we believe it or not, it is there for all of us to help ourselves to.

Knowledge comes in different packages, with different labels, in different sizes and seemingly from different sources, and yet there is only one source. Knowing this will put us on the right track instantly because there is so much to know. It all depends on what journey we have chosen to be on. Everything else will fall into our path.

We notice how babies, as soon as they open their eyes to this world, want to know and search with their eyes and want to touch things. When they start crawling, they investigate everything within reach. When they can talk, they are in an ocean of questions. In fact, we hear parents saying how their children never stop asking questions. There is a thirst for learning in children that surpasses that of adults. Some keep that thirst to know more and more all their lives. Others are content with not learning much. Most will learn as much as they need in order to live in the society they are in and at the level they have chosen.

We are all learning constantly, with awareness or without. We could be focusing on subjects we choose or struggling with those chosen for us. We may have access to elite private education or follow the main stream. There are those with no access to any formal education whatsoever. They have to use nature and whatever is around them to learn. If they are lucky they may find great natural teachers who fill them with precious knowledge.

From a very early age we already know who we want to be in life, and our dreams are awake. Situations and circumstances can change our dreams and send us on different roads. Often we may return to our original dream. It could be that we are good at another way of learning. With each individual there is a new way of learning and teaching, and as we learn we teach others. Learning and teaching do not just happen in schools and universities. Learning is all around us our whole lives. Travelling around the world and actually spending time with people from different backgrounds will teach much more than sitting in a school reading, memorising and discussing how those people live.

Books are precious. They have information to motivate us and inform us in so many ways on our journey. However, we learn best from what we experience, how we interpret it and the use we make of it. Our best teachings are those that come from having experienced them ourselves. Learning and teaching go hand in hand. We may have been at a lecture and not got anything out of it, but a few words from another student made it clear.

The best knowledge is that which comes from within us, when we allow ourselves to be our real true selves. When we trust the treasures in our knowledge, our insights become important. We keep finding clues all the way to put us in positions of experiencing what our insights dictate. We cannot but marvel at our findings, how we come across them and how things evolve around us so that this knowledge becomes our reality. It may be that was what we came to find and to do here on planet earth.

A WORLD THAT MOVES FAST

Our world started to move faster and faster years ago and now it goes at a very rapid speed. Everything seems to be changing faster. Changes are taking place in disconcerting ways and many people worry but do not know what to do. We are approaching the biggest change for thousands of years and we do not see the population at large prepared for it. It could be out of ignorance, disbelief or not wanting to move out of their comfort zones.

Individuals and groups from different fronts are warning us about the big change that will occur in the near future. They all talk about events that will take place on earth and how to prepare for them. They tell us that the planet will be divided and it is up to us on which part of it we want to be. If we are awake we will move with Gaia (Mother Earth) to a higher dimension. If we are still sleeping and do not want to wake up, we will have the alternative to stay on the same three-dimensional conditions we have now.

I would like to believe there is still time for people to change their minds as to which side they want to be on. However, there is some work to do. If we want to stay with the third dimension we carry on being as we are. If we want to go higher, then there are layers of debris we need to remove from our past experiences in this life and past lives; the quicker we start the better, as time is pressing now. Those of us who have always known we wanted to go with Gaia have been working on it for many years. However, because of this rapid change of Gaia and the Light it enjoys at the moment, everything is becoming easier and faster. Therefore, everything is possible if we have the right intention, vibrating it with passion and allowing it to manifest.

We are told that if we stay with the third dimension we will carry on with the same problems: wars, dark energies of hate, anger, greed, envy, jealousy, to name but a few; fighting and struggling to live. On the other hand, they say that if we go to higher dimensions we will have peace and wellbeing. All the problems and unpleasantness we lived through in the third dimension will not be there any more. The choice is ours.

If we decided to go with Gaia, we would have to work on our personal development by going into our inner selves and doing a very good cleansing. Working from the heart. Opening up and allowing our inner true Self to guide us through all the entanglements and misconceptions acquired over so many past years.

They have been telling us for years that all the help we may think we need is in us and we can deal with anything we are presented with. We have reached a time now when there will not be saviours coming to rescue us, because we have the power to rescue ourselves. We only have to believe it and allow it. The Supreme Universal Intelligence will do the rest.

We very much hope that by the time the split takes place we will all be happy with the decisions we have made. We are grateful to Source for the support we have constantly in order to reach our highest potential in every way possible.

DIGGING INTO OURSELVES

We are always surprised at what we find when we go deep into ourselves. The depth has no end, and yet we are connected to that infinity. As we remove layers that are obstructing our way, we go deeper and deeper into what is holding us back.

Earlier on in our search, each time we successfully moved unwanted energies, we thought our job was done and felt relieved. Somehow it soon appeared we had to go on clearing and digging. In those early days we thought it was impossible to dissolve so much from ourselves individually, and somehow knew we were probably part of the crew to cleanse whatever was around us.

We clear energies we are attached to from previous experiences in different time lines. The thing is that there are so many lines that it seems we never finish. When our intention is to clear energies that are blocking us, it is interesting to observe that the Universal Intelligence is guiding us so we can find them easily, and thus it gives us the opportunity to free ourselves from them. It happens in uncountable and surprising ways, which makes it difficult to explain the fact that each of us is shown the path which only we can understand, at whatever level we are at. So if we were to present someone with the prompts that another individual has had, that someone would not be able to make sense of it. Yet for the individual who has originally received those prompts it is natural and easy to follow.

Even though we can be open minded about what we may receive, we are always surprised by the canny ways we muddle through, in order to remove energies we did not even know we had or that we had to remove. If we want to clear something, it is because it is not pleasant to us. In the same way, the prompts we receive usually come through unpleasantness and feelings of discomfort. However, as we move on, the prompts become lighter and subtler. The only inconvenience is that, if we are not aware and mindful, we miss the prompts and therefore we remain stationary - in other words, stuck. Being in awareness pays off, because we are in tune with our higher Self and able to follow its guidance and thus reach our objectives.

The main point here is not to take anything for granted in our lives, especially our feelings. Our feelings are like torches lighting our path in darkness. Paying attention to our feelings, we can move smoothly along even the roughest of roads. At times, feelings can be strong and we cannot miss them. But other times they can be extremely subtle and not relevant to anything that may be happening at any particular time in our lives. So, for our own wellbeing, it is in our interest to be attentive and aware.

One important thing to bear in mind is that whatever we do to ourselves we do to the world, and whatever we do to others we do to ourselves. It is in our interest to understand this.

The deeper we dig in, the higher our vibrations become. One clue is that feelings become repetitive, and that draws our attention to the fact that there is something beneath them.

Awareness, alertness and meditation are our tools for success.

OUR STRENGTHS AND WEAKNESSES

. . . .

Our strengths are abundant and powerful. Our weaknesses are fewer, and they only become powerful when our strengths allow it.

We are born with all our powers in place. When we become aware we are in a physical body that restricts us from doing and undoing with the speed and efficiency we are used to, our strengths and weaknesses become alive in us, even though we may not remember later in life.

We are strong and powerful beings. Our biggest weakness is that we do not believe it, and therefore we create an open gate for other weaknesses to come in all through our lives. From there on, we can search every aspect of our lives and see the internal battles we have with ourselves fighting these two powers. If we were to allow honesty to speak for us without influences of any kind, we would see how circumstances were and are managed by these battles. We are our own enemies, although we look for our enemies outside ourselves. No wonder we find ourselves lost again and again, because we are looking in the wrong places. A lot of people, when they are told that the solution to their lives or problems is in them, refuse to accept it or believe it. They carry on as they were before, even though they know their ways are not working for them. Some people do stop and think. They listen to those who went ahead of them and know ways to the path they are looking for, and they are eager to wake up to who they really are.

Even those who are advanced in this knowledge and those who know about balancing both sides well, so as not to fall on the weak side, must remain actively aware as the weakness is watching and ready to move in when the opportunity presents itself. This can happen because of many things: tiredness, laziness, being caught in a net of superfluous charm, having the wrong illusion in their minds, thinking it will be without consequence, just to mention a few. These situations can repeat themselves, and their consequences are tough. Why do they keep happening again and again? We suffer through this lack of firm determination. We are like a weak tree, which bends with the slightest breeze. We want to be like a strong oak that no hurricane can bend.

Have you been in situations where you are doing or thinking something that does not fit in you and it makes you feel uncomfortable, but you are still going ahead with it? If you feel that, the best thing is to check if you are allowing your weaknesses to take over and ask yourself why you are doing it. What gates have you opened to these weaknesses? And, what gates have you opened to your strengths? Then, see where you stand in your life. What is active? What is passive? To which side do you give more attention? Which do you enjoy most? Now, examine the enjoyment. Is it blissful and lasting? Or is it exciting, tiring and short lived? The choice is always yours. Whatever your life is, it is what you have made. You are the only one who can change your life. Reflecting on life gives us a lot of clues. Meditation allows us to be in touch with our true Self and aware of our strengths. Believing in our strengths, our weaknesses will remain weak.

EMOTIONS

· ·

Most of us, if not all, are run by emotions of one kind or other. What are emotions? How do they come to be? Have we ever looked into why they are there? Are we aware how their power can move us and the world around?

Emotions are transitory and follow our deepest thoughts. Emotions are in constant movement and change their energy frequency constantly at the speed and density of the thought they are following. Of course, we have a great diversity of thoughts that are like light emissions we throw out into space. It would be impossible to manifest all those thoughts in our physical state. The emotions follow those deep, strong thoughts. The powers with which we project those thoughts give way to the emotions we feel. Even when we have no emotions, this still comes from the projection of our thoughts.

Emotions are driven by our way of thinking. When something excites us, our thoughts accelerate when we want to express this excitement. When we lose something or someone we love, our thoughts plunge us into missing what has been lost. When we have achieved something important for ourselves or we have met someone special, we leap into the air with joy. When we are stuck in traffic, a good friend has betrayed us, we lose our job, we are ill, or a relative is ill, our feelings keep changing. In every instance, and many others that life offers, if we observe our thoughts we will see how the emotions we feel are exactly matched to the thoughts we are having. This observation is of the most importance, because it gives us the awareness that if we change our thoughts, we can change our emotions and therefore our degree of sadness or joy, excitement or dullness, or whatever other emotion is in the air for us.

We are under the impression that other people have to love us in order for us to be loved. This is a myth. Examining this myth, we will find that it is a misleading thought in most people and comes directly via our thinking. We do not need to be loved by other people, because we ARE love. Our real identity is love and joy. Whether we want to believe and accept it or not, it is not going to change that fact. Once this is clear in our minds, we realise that we can make ourselves happy with or without anyone else being involved, since we are that amazing power that we keep denying ourselves. Awakening to this reality brings us closer to our true Self and to our role here on planet earth.

There are already individuals who have discovered that we can use our mind to command a machine just like a remote control. That is part of our reality coming and manifesting itself in ways which we cannot deny.

What are emotions? Asking this question and letting it be, the answer will come sooner or later, depending in how ready we are to receive it. Meanwhile, here is our version of it. Emotions are the direct product of our thoughts. Change our thoughts and the emotions will follow. It is clear that the rudder is in our hands, and as always it is up to us. The choice is ours. It is not controlling: rather, it is changing and allowing our true selves to take charge of our lives.

LIMITATIONS

. . . .

Some people are limited without knowing they are. Others treat their limitations as traditions, ways they learned from parents and ancestors, and they therefore feel proud to follow them. There are some who are limited by those above them; it could be parents, teachers, and superiors in any category, at work or through their financial situation. We can also have physical, mental and character limitations.

As children, generally speaking, our parents stop us from doing vital things that come naturally to us and which are beyond the comprehension of our parents. Ironically, that is why they stop us from doing things, not realising that they are cutting and damaging our wings, altering our flight in our journey. This will be the biggest of our limitations, because from there on most of us will become reserved, and fearful to express what comes to us naturally. This equals limitations.

When we grow up to the age we can decide for ourselves and be responsible for our own actions, it is then that quite a lot of people move on to do what they always wanted to do and excel at it. There are those who still feel the wounds of their cut wings and cannot quite take off. They will find limitations everywhere. There are the ones among us who were indoctrinated or brainwashed with the dos and don'ts imposed by those who brought us up, educated us, or both. There are those who, through the positions and jobs they do, are put down by their bosses and treated badly, and the result of this is ending up with further cuts to their wings and mutilation of their dreams, which equals limitations.

There are the followers of traditions who follow religiously what they have seen at home, hearing that was the way. They feel virtuous in keeping up the traditions, forgetting they are stuck without novelty and are not moving forward in time and with the world.

The most severe of the limitations are those imposed by ourselves through fear, anxiety or lack of self-esteem. With the other types of limitations, we are on the lookout for opportunities to get out of the limit zones. However, if we have created our own limitations, how do we get out of them? In most cases, we do not know we are limited. We just live whatever lives we live. We make our mind up that life has given it to us, and that is all there is to it. But that is not so.

No matter what our situations are from childhood to adulthood, we do not have to be limited in any way. We are always free from within to fly against all the odds, no matter what. We are powerful beings regardless of the situations we find ourselves in. There are infinite ways waiting for us to use. It is good to remember that most of the difficulties we encounter were designed by us for us to experience them and therefore learn what there is to learn from them. The greater the difficulty, the greater the lesson. Bearing this in mind will keep us centred, strong, and free from limitations.

We are limitless beings in physical bodies that limit us in the physical world, but we can use our power to go beyond the limits. This has been proven over and over again by those whose achievements the world marvels at. We all came with the power to achieve whatever we projected to do. So any blockages or limits in our way can be dissolved.

LACK OF AWARENESS

· ·

Lack of awareness can handicap us in many ways. Most times we do not realise we have been handicapped, so we do not do anything about situations that are under our noses: we are blind to them until they reach a degree where we are forced to see them, but by then a lot of damage has been done and not all of it can be repaired.

Being aware is an essential skill, which takes us from the simplest of things to the most deep and profound to be found in our existence on earth. Awareness is indispensable if we want the best for ourselves and the whole world. Awareness is achievable and it is at hand.

There are so many times in so many of us, when we can see what is happening in our day to day life. It does not resonate with what is in our hearts, but we do not do anything about it. We carry on as if we had not noticed anything. Unfortunately, the consequences are hard to take. The question to ask here is: why do we not want to stop and examine what is happening in our lives and the responses we get from our hearts? Even so, situations can be difficult at times as life goes on. We can go on and on for years, exhausting our resources physically and at all levels, handicapping ourselves by denying ourselves the right to be true to who we are, true to our Self.

The planet is changing rapidly and so is life on it. There is a lot of movement as the Universe wants to put us all in place, and as always, there are choices to be made. This is when being aware is important so that we make the right choices.

Some years ago, after a workshop, someone approached us and asked what was "awareness". At that time, this word was not used as much as it is today. Fortunately, the awakening of the masses into other ways of seeing life is taking place very fast now. Also, there are so many people in the world saying the same things, that even those who may have certain doubts can reassure themselves by comparing notes from country to country, where people speak different languages and do not know each other, yet they are saying the same things. We have observed how, in the different cultures around the world, we have the same wise sayings to guide us or to help us understand certain situations. It shows how close we are, even though in appearance it does not seem so. The mere fact of reflecting on this will take us a long way towards awakening our awareness within us. We have all the tools and all the knowledge; we just have to want that reality and the denial will go away.

If awareness is not with us, we are not in the present moment. We get there by being alert, by examining frequently how we feel, by being mindful of what is around us and how we react to it, by observing how others behave towards us and in our circles, by paying attention to what is going on in our lives and the world as a whole, by spending a lot of time in our own company and being in close relationship with our hearts, by listening carefully to what our hearts have to say and acting accordingly, by loving, respecting and honouring ourselves before anyone else and watching the miracle of all that flowing out into the world as a strong energy that binds us together with those particular qualities of love, respect and honour.

Meditation encourages awareness.

VOLUNTARY WORK

When we volunteer to do work or help others, why do we do it? What is our purpose? Who asked us to do it? These are important questions to ask ourselves in order to be effective in what we do.

We have seen very keen volunteers driven by their belief that they have to do voluntary work in order to progress in their spiritual path. Their attitude defies the cause, because they see themselves superior to those they help. We have seen volunteers helping out of duty in different forms, family, church, community or country. Others do it to fill in their own emptiness or shut down the noises of their own minds. Then, there are those who are the real volunteers, who work with their hearts filled with unconditional love, free from duties or personal needs. They are the real volunteers: the ones who will make a difference to those they are helping by touching them with the power of love, and not out of duty or selfish gain.

Before we offer to do voluntary work, we would have to check and make sure we are in the right condition to do it. It is vital that we have within us what we want to offer. We cannot offer love if we do not love ourselves. We cannot suggest ways of making things work if we do not do it ourselves. We cannot teach something we do not practise. We cannot ask anyone to be honest if we are not honest ourselves. The idea is that we must have the strength we are offering inside us to really make a difference. We could say that something is better than nothing. The point here is to work on ourselves and replace the weaknesses with strengths, become unshakable, do whatever we do out of pure love, and care for ourselves because as we give to others we are giving to ourselves. In other words, by taking care of ourselves we are taking care of others too. Our vibrations of wellbeing and the skills we may have will lift anyone in need. However, if we ourselves are in need we can only add more to their needs. So let us bring ourselves to the awareness of our actions and be mindful of what we are doing.

When we really understand how to give help or undertake voluntary work is after we have experienced needs in our own lives. Sometimes these have been met and others not. Needs can become bigger through the help received.

We are not putting off volunteers. They should just check and be aware of the situations they are going to tackle. Nobody is perfect. We may not be ready in certain areas, but we may be in others. So by choosing and approaching volunteering in fields we are proficient at and we can control, we will be great helpers. Certain things are essential: a big heart full of unconditional love and free from pity but full of compassion, knowing that the help we may give is not for the others but for us, enjoying what we do so the helped ones perceive that joy and it gives them hope.

We may not be aware of how much we depend on each other. We are all helpers and being helped in one way or another. The most perfect help, from where we perceive it, is when we visualise everyone with the power to overcome anything that comes along and touches their lives, and by seeing them thriving in what they love doing.

A big thank you to all volunteers with unconditional loving hearts.

HELPING OTHERS

. . . .

We all feel inclined to give a hand to others when we are in situations where our help is needed and we can give it. When this happens there is a deep inner feeling of wellbeing, which many will call satisfaction for helping. We would call it relief.

There are many associations and charities in the world for helping people, at home and in other countries, mainly manned by volunteers. If we look around we see an amazing volunteering network. We find groups in churches, schools, hospitals, communities and across the nation. Anyone can start a group according to the interests they may have and the needs they may see. Also, they may want to help others through experiences they may have had themselves. So there is a long list of things to choose from if you wish to help.

Things we hear from volunteers: *"Helping others makes me feel so good, and those people I help are so appreciative."* *"When I did not know what to do or where to turn, I saw they were looking for volunteers in the community so I went along for lack of a better thing to do and I started helping there. Now I feel changed. My life has turned around. I feel renewed, thanks to helping others."* *"When we joined the programme 'médecins sans frontières' and worked for 6 months abroad without the right equipment and with desperate people, that made a difference in our lives."* *"When we have someone at the other end of the line saying they want to end their life and we manage to prevent that from happening by just being there with them and giving them our time, the feeling we get is one of relief and gratefulness."*

How about you? Have you volunteered at any time of your life? How could you help others? How could you be helped? A woman told us that she was feeling so unhappy and with nothing to do that she felt like helping others. Then, she thought: what could she offer in her condition? One day she plucked up courage and went along to offer her time. She said that was the best day of her life. She felt so good and appreciated and her heart felt full of love. We can only see the value of our actions once we have immersed ourselves in the job and see what can be done.

Volunteering is a feeling that comes from the heart with compassion and dedication. We give our time willingly and feel very good about it. Expecting something in exchange becomes a business transaction. There is joy in us when we see we have made a difference, even though it could be a small one, given our perception of the world, but not for those we have helped. We always feel connected through the heart to those we help. If we search, deep down we are helping ourselves all the time, whether we are aware of it or not. If we care to examine our feelings to the very roots, we will find what brought us to where we are and what we are doing. We are all able to do this process. If you do not know how to do it, look for guidance.

There are those who give money to charities that is much needed and appreciated. That way of giving has no comparison to what we are talking about, where we give our time and take part full-heartedly in whatever action we have chosen to be involved in. There are those who give money to the charities they support and also take part in their activities. They surely feel great for it.

It is good to remember that everything we do for others, in reality we are doing for ourselves.

TRANSFORMING ENERGIES

For some years now we have heard children talking about "Transformers". There have been all kinds of Transformer toys and films on the subject of transforming machines that do many different things according to what they have been transformed into. When we are connected to children, we are always learning.

Transforming is a familiar word related to the flow of changing energies and the frequency with which they come into our awareness. We tell those who ask us how easy it is to change energies we do not want and are not serving us any more. The simplicity of it makes people doubt it. That is why it is good to watch children at play to learn how simple it is to turn what seems impossible into possible. We can do that kind of transformation in our real life.

There is a TED Talk where the speaker tells how the events in his life made him powerfully angry. That anger was destroying him. He realised it and decided to transform the power of anger he was feeling into something that would help the people in his community. To his surprise, it worked. He changed his community for the better and started to extend his skills to other communities. He was proud of his achievement.

If you ever have an energy that is bothering you, you can transform it into a different one that you feel happier with. It is that simple. We can do it by connecting with our heart and allowing the transformation to take place.

It is important to be connected and aligned to Source, so we can follow the guidance we receive. If we feel uncomfortable with negative feelings, for example anger, sadness, guilt, loneliness, fear, anxiety and so on, we do not have to feel those energies because we can change them for joy, gratefulness, enthusiasm, interest in life and what it has to offer us, and the whole abundance of things there are to satisfy our choices.

We can transform whatever is in ourselves, and we can help others to do the same. Awareness is the key, and being mindful of how we feel is what helps to turn the key into making a difference to the world and ourselves.

Paying attention to our feelings will make us great performers for the good of all. Bearing in mind that what we think and do vibrates through the whole universe, affecting those whose wavelengths are in tune with our own, and therefore making a difference in many ways, one of which could be transforming energies for the better of us all.

If you have your children around you, grandchildren, a relative's children or any children, then observe them at play and listen to what they say. They are more connected and aligned with Source than many adults, and there is a great deal to learn from them.

Let us be great Transformers, enjoy life and everything in it. Let us observe the transformation of nature with each season. We are part of nature too. If we drop our resistances we will be successful Transformers.

LISTENING SKILLS

. . . .

We all hear, but not all of us listen. How many times do people hear but have no idea of what has been said to them? They heard the sounds of the words void of meaning because their attention was not on what they were hearing. This lack of presence gives way to many misunderstandings that could be avoided by being in the present moment. Do we allow the person speaking to us to speak without interruptions? Our lack of patience in listening is enough proof that we do not have that skill.

Have we asked ourselves how our listening skills are? Have we judged others for not listening to us? And when we listen, how do we do it? Where is our mind? Where is our attention? Are we thinking or doing other things at the same time as listening? A self-assessment on this subject will serve us to be more whole and efficient in what we do. If we think of how many misunderstandings there have been in our lives and how many were rooted in the wrong interpretation of words not heard or listened to appropriately, we will find many unpleasant situations which could have been avoided by simply listening skilfully.

It is important to spend some time observing what we do when we are listening to others. Are we listening with our hearts or are we listening with our intellect? The answer to these questions will tell us what to expect from our listening. When we listen with our heart, we connect with the person we are listening to and we can easily tell if they are genuine or not in what they are saying. Sometimes they want us to believe what they are saying, but what they have in mind in reality is very different. When we work with a clear heart, we are able to communicate with that clarity that comes from it. If the heart is charged with emotions, no matter what they may be, then the heart cannot communicate with the freedom required for a successful outcome.

When we listen with our intellect, we are in a different world altogether. The mind takes over with all its tendencies.

In our experience, when we listen with the heart there is no need for words. Words become cumbersome. Communication from heart to heart is direct, clear and with the speed of light, and no misunderstandings ever take place. There are no teachings for this type of communication. We are born with this skill. If through life we have lost it, we can find it by removing the layers obstructing it.

When we listen from the heart we can help many people in many different ways. Our own technique is listening with the heart. Sometimes, it would mean the absence of words and being in the silence of the two hearts communicating. Without having uttered a word we can resolve the most complicated issues.

In a world of noises, it is impossible to be silent. However, we can find our inner silence anywhere, regardless of surroundings and distractions. Our most important listening is to ourselves. Listening attentively to our heart and allowing it to guide us is the clue to a better and more successful life, because we are in our centre and communicating directly with our inner selves.

WE ARE POWERFUL BEINGS

Most humans have forgotten how powerful they are. There are others who feel the power vibrating in them but they are not clear where it comes from. There are those who feel it in ways that do not support or serve them or society. There are those who feel it and want more of it but do not know how to go about it. There are some who are looking for the roots of it all and do it in different ways. There are those who know and take it upon themselves to enlighten others. There are also the already enlightened ones, who teach the latter ones to do the job well.

Our ancestors were looking for saviours because they could not see through the density of the energies they were living through. Apparently, we inherited quite a lot of that and with it the habits established through generations. One generation passed this on to the next until it reached ours. If we listen to astrologers, they explain to us how everything changes and how this is the time when the planet earth is due to change. Those in the spiritual realms will explain to us that the planet has reached her cycle and is changing to move into a different one of light and wellbeing.

We are now in a powerful moment as part of this creation. We have had many lives in it, all of them different in every aspect possible. Now the planet is changing, taking those who are awake to a place of light, peace and wellbeing, very different to what we have now. The choice is there for all. Those who are still sleeping and attached to the old ways will carry on living the same kind of experiences they have now. The choice is personal. Nobody can force anyone to change or even to awaken. There are a lot of people around helping those who want to be awake. You only need the desire to be awake and help will come your way. However, you will have to be open to that help.

What are we awakening to? To be awake is to know we are powerful beings, very powerful, more than we can imagine. It means we are not in need of saviours any more because we are our own saviours. This is a new beginning. The past must be left behind if we want to move on with the light. To be awake is to remember we are energy and can only ascend if our energy is light and love, joy and wellbeing. The other energy, where people believe the life they are living in this physical world is their reality, is dense and cannot ascend unless they wake up. So it will stay behind.

One thing to be aware of is that these changes are taking place very rapidly already, to the point that those who are ascending can see their thoughts being manifested straight away. That makes us aware of our own truth. Our true Self is showing us the way to what we can do.

All it takes is to know how powerful we are. We are part of the Universal Intelligence that controls worlds and universes. It controls us, but allows us to have the choice to be on one side or the other. It is part of the contrasts of life. You can be good or bad. You can be in darkness or light. You can be happy or sad. It is all a question of choices, and we decide which one to take. There is no right or wrong. Whatever you decide is the right thing for you at this time. You may need more experiences before you decide to ascend to a more peaceful life.

EVERYTHING IS POSSIBLE

. . . .

Everything is possible when our limitations are not in the way. How do we know that? Very simply, by observing our thoughts, behaviour, habits, resistances, feelings and, above all, fears. All these will be good indicators for us to know where we are at in knowing ourselves well and how able we are to perform or manifest those things that seem impossible.

Some of us have experienced and are experiencing amazing achievements. Some people are well known for it. Others are not known to the masses but are just as important for themselves and those around them. If we were to examine our lives in depth, we would find heroic achievements that on the surface may seem to be of no consequence, but in reality are very important to us and our communities.

Have you ever been overwhelmed by your own achievements? Have you ever watched people doing incredible things that you would not have thought of doing even in your imagination? And there is the clue. Not thinking about it does not take us anywhere. We have to think first with purpose. We all have the same power. It depends how we want to use it. It depends if we are careful not to give it away to others or allow others to take it from us.

There are many ways in which our power can be stolen from us, so it is important to be alert to whom we are dealing with. Common situations where this happens are: within families, under threats, abusive behaviour, making people believe they are worthless and so on.

When we are connected to our true Self, we are always safe. Even so, we may go through difficult situations. The point here is how we deal with them. We have to remember at all times that we are projections with a particular programme. We were the ones who created the programme and wanted to be in these experiences, no matter how hard it may be for us now to believe we could have ever wanted those things in our lives. It does not matter whether we accept the fact or not. What we did is not going to change just because we do not believe it. Whatever our programme may be, we have the power to change it. What for some people are struggles in life for others are adventures. It all depends on the approach we have to what is in front of us.

Whatever we may have found impossible in the past is not the case anymore. Everything is possible. We think it and it can manifest without us doing anything physically. It is already happening. Sceptics will have a hard time with this. They are the ones who are still sleeping and not ready to move on to an easier world.

Our power is beyond measure. We can do anything we wish with it. It is up to us what we do. Nobody can do it for us. If someone offers to do it, they are taking our power away from us. We are the sole co-creators of our lives. We programmed it before coming to the planet and we can make changes if need be. When we meditate we feel our power alive in us.

Everything is possible when we know and believe in who we are.

EGO

. . . .

What is ego? What does it do to us? Do we check it regularly to make sure that it works for us and not against us? We often hear people talking about the ego of others and seldom about their own.

Our ego is essential for us to know who we are on the planet and in society and enthuse us into pushing up in our profession and as a person, so as to become the best we can be. The other side of ego is not so helpful to us if we do not have it under control. However, if we are aware of it at all times, it is manageable.

We come across people who think that ego is just a kind of arrogance, and that is a pitfall for many. Ego has many faces and subtleties, and that is why so many can be fooled by it. Ego is boisterous but can be very shy. It can play the victim in order to seek attention. It can be a show-off. Ego-driven people often lack sensitivity and can hurt others, and even feel good about it. They can be loud. They can be refined. They can be unscrupulous and unkind. They think about themselves and their own interests in a kind of selfish way, not taking into account how others around them can be affected. It can be so subtle at times that it goes undetected and it can even be taken for something nice and helpful.

Watching out for our ego and having it under control is advantageous to us because we are avoiding conflicts in our lives. As we do that, we can also see other people's ego and that puts us on guard, making sure we do not play their game. That way we avoid a lot of trouble.

It can be painful to watch some people tear themselves apart because of their ego. But it is still more painful to suffer the consequences of it in us. Ego can block us and stop us from doing what we really want.

It is with amazement we watch the never-ending ego battles people have. Often they are not aware of them. Ego has canny ways of creating difficult situations and making us act without us realising it.

When our attention goes to the ego of anyone and we notice it clearly, sometimes we even criticise it. This would be a good way of finding our own ego. We see what we have in us reflected in other people. If we are good observers we can see in others all those things that are within ourselves. This gives us a chance to correct them. Sometimes there are contradictions or conflicts which, although unpleasant at the time they are happening, are blessings in disguise, because they bring to the forefront issues we could not otherwise see, and it gives us the opportunity to resolve them.

It helps to bear in mind the fact that we are all the same energy and we all have the same facilities of being great, as well as being anything else. It all comes from the same source, whether it is good or bad. We choose it by having our attention and vibration on it. If we attach too much attention to wanting to control the ego, we will only make it bigger, because we are feeding it rather than removing it. Using our naturalness will keep away the unwanted ego.

DOUBTS

• •

Are you a person who tends to doubt? Are you aware of the nature of your doubts? Have you thought about where your doubts come from? If so, what are their origins? When we look closer at our doubts, we are amazed at what we find out about ourselves.

The variety of doubts and the degree in which they present themselves to us depend mainly on the kind of person we are, and also where we are in society, the job we hold and the life we have in general. All of this can reflect on the kind of doubts we have.

A lot of doubts are born out of our insecurity, lack of trust, lack of knowledge, lack of worth, lack of knowing who we are, lack of proof of something or other. If we are loaded with one or more of these, they will become the basis for other doubts and will attract more doubts of all kinds.

Doubts in any kind of relationship are very damaging. Doubts in what we do or projects we may have will cause failure. When doubting something we are not giving it a chance to be. When doubting someone we are not giving them permission to unfold in a natural way. When we doubt ourselves we are sabotaging our own lives. Doubts are like the brakes of a car: they stop us from going forward and keep us stuck wherever we may be.

Let us take two athletes. One is a good runner but has doubts about winning the race. The other is not so good but believes he will win the race. The second one will win the race because he has not put his brakes on. He just runs convinced of winning, while the first one, even though he has everything in his favour, loses because his doubts slow him down.

Doubts can make businesses fail and prevent dreams from coming true, issues from being resolved, illnesses from healing, and so on. It is what we put in our minds that will manifest. The reason some people are thought of as being lucky is more because, free from doubts, they put their attention on what they want.

Eliminating the roots of our doubts will eliminate our doubts. It is like pulling up a tree: the tree will disappear. If, instead, we cut its branches, the tree will keep growing more branches. That is why it is important to find out where the roots are and what causes them to exist, in order to remove the doubts from our lives.

If we have doubts and are prepared to look into how to remove them, the first step is to know that by just having the intention to do it, we will find the ways that suit us best. The rest is up to us, provided we allow it and trust ourselves.

Being free from doubts will change any life and will give freedom to do what we want with clarity and peace of mind. It will save time and give quality to your life. We can all do it. We all have the same power to do it. It is a question of being brave and taking the first step. We are blessed.

WHAT WE TELL OURSELVES

hat we tell ourselves sometimes, or a lot of the time, is far from being true, and we are quite blind to this fact. We even give ourselves reasons to support what we think in order to make it believable. This usually comes out of our low self-esteem or expectations we may have.

There are different ways of understanding people and situations from our own standpoint. We tend to stand on a point that suits us and where we have gradually grown accustomed to being. From there we look around our immediate world such as family, friends, neighbours and colleagues, and the situations that could arise with them all. Our perception of their roles in our lives comes to be affected by whatever our moods are and these are in constant change, so they are not reliable. Examining our position and bearing in mind our moods and the charge they may carry will give us clarity in whatever situation we may be in.

Have you had thoughts about friends or even family who do not show much interest in you, and you assume they do not like you as much as before? When these thoughts come to your mind, have you considered the many possible reasons why their reactions are not as they were before? Have you asked yourself where you are in relation to whom or what you are passing judgement on? Where are you? What is your standpoint? How did you get there? How do you perceive things compared to the way you did before? How different is your standpoint now compared to before? Do you take into account all the changes in you and everyone else around you?

Misunderstandings occur frequently in relationships for the simplest of things. We can ask ourselves questions like those above, or similar ones, to clarify in our minds our position at the time we were wondering: why have others changed or not changed the way they look at us or the way they behave with us? Then we would see that in the majority of cases it is not them but us who have changed. This would open for us the option of changing our mood and perception and stepping into the harmony of time and the changes that go with it. People with low self-esteem or those wanting perfection in themselves and in others may fall into this trap of seeing the world in just one colour, when in reality there are many colours.

We can see lost friendships and how members of families distance themselves one from another by imaginary thoughts and stories they tell themselves that are not true at all. They have not changed; we have changed our perception of them. These imaginary stories can bring suffering and unpleasantness. Examining ourselves with loving care, free of judgement and with honesty allows us to accept our weaknesses and convert them into strengths. Looking inside ourselves, we are not only removing layers that are blocking our sight, but we are able to see our real treasure hidden in the depth of our heart.

By examining our thoughts, perceptions and standpoints free from judgement we are eliminating obstacles and creating clarity in our lives without the need to judge or criticise others. This gives us the pleasure of enjoying our friends and family as we have always done, and we adjust to their changes the same way we adjust to our own, bearing in mind that if ours prove to be difficult at times, so will theirs. Unconditional love is the key to keeping harmony among us all.

CLUES THAT HELP US

W e are given clues all along our way in many forms and shapes. Some are very easy to pick up and we can see them immediately. We are slower at recognising others and it can take us months or years to find out that they are there as clues to help us.

Let us look at some examples:

- Whenever we sat down to do a particular thing, we had an itch on the rear left side of our ribs. We found it uncomfortable because we could not shake it off and could not scratch it either. After over three months we realised that the itch was connected to something we had been working on, which needed a different approach. That done, the itch went.

- There was a child who we could not stand. We looked and looked for reasons for this strong dislike and what we could find was not reason enough to have such a reaction to the child. After eight years we found there were energies from past lives that needed to be cleared. We were very grateful to that child who presented features before us that made us react so strongly that we had to work on ourselves.

- We had information about a certain person. Without knowing the person, we immediately felt a dislike towards him. When we were asked if we wanted to meet him, our NO was categorical. The feeling of dislike was strongly charged. There were no reasons we could find for it. Again, there were past lives unresolved and now we had opportunities to resolve them.

- When we are at the door about to go out, there is a feeling in us that makes us stop for a moment as if in doubt of something. We close the door and leave, to find out later that we have left behind an important item we needed. This can happen in different forms. We can find ourselves in a room not knowing why we are there. We come out and go to another room where we are going to work, and find out we need something that was in the first room without knowing why. These are easy clues and happen frequently to most people.

- Nature gives us many clues. Shrubs, trees and flowers can change our perception so that we see what our next step is according to the situation we are in.
- Even something we see on the floor as we go to meet someone can warn us of what we will find and so we can be ready for it. In the same way, it can be any other thing that attracts our attention, and we allow our intuition to tell us what the meaning of it is.
- When watching a film or a television programme and one of the characters stands out for us and we like or dislike them, it is giving us a clue. We have cleared a lot through these clues. This can be found in people we pass in the street and do not know.

These are just a few examples. However, we must bear in mind that clues always come to us in ways we can understand, even if it takes time for us to recognise them. They will be different for each of us.

WHEN WE ARE WORRIED

Most people always seem to be worrying about something. It is part of their life. It is a way to keep the mind occupied without them realising it. It is incredible how many things people choose to be worried about, and they share their worries with all their many friends and relations. How about you? Are you one of them? Do you have worries? What are your worries?

When we worry we forget we are mortals and we do not know when our time will be over. We forget that we may not be here tomorrow or the day after. Therefore every minute counts. We came to live our lives to the maximum and not to waste time on worrying or any other negative energy. When we are aware, we are alert about these things not being in our lives because we realise that worrying is using our good energy to bring us what we do not want.

Worrying is the opposite of being connected to Source. When we are disconnected, we become vulnerable and we feel our world moves in ways we cannot control or comprehend. So we worry without thinking of the consequences it can cause. Another thing we do when we worry is that we have our attention on what we are worrying about, which will give strength to the problem and also to our worry. One thing we hear a lot is "I try to get it out of my head but it won't go". "Trying" is keeping us stuck. The way of changing a stubborn thought is by changing it for a pleasant one. That will decrease the strength of the unwanted thought and increase that of the wanted one, reaching a point where the unwanted thought will go completely. There is another way of clearing the mind. When we know who we are and how we can create what we have, then we will realise that the same way we create it, we can also eliminate it.

Worrying can surprise us when we least expect it and that can throw us out of our centre. It is disconcerting, and for the time it lasts we feel quite lost, not knowing which way to turn or what to do. By bringing our attention back to our centre we regain control and the solutions are at hand. We can move in the right direction with confidence.

Quietening the mind and being in silence will take us back to our centre easily. When we remove the doer and allow our inner guidance to be in place, all will be well.

When we get up every morning, we are thankful for another day and see the possibilities we have ahead to enjoy the day. Being at all times conscious of the fact that our body is impermanent and has a limited time of life on the planet will change our perspectives and how we feel. So our aim is to profit as much as we can from every minute we spend here. Everything we do is accountable to our true Self which is permanent and will go back to the non-physical world with the experiences gained in the physical one.

It is important at all times to remember that it is in our hands to change the way we feel no matter what. It is up to us if we feel miserable or joyful, "poor me" or courageous, strong or weak. Situations also change when we change our thoughts and ways of seeing them. It is up to us to take the direction that suits us. We have the power and guidance for it at all times. Waking up to it is finding who we really are.

THE JOY OF THE HEART

. . . .

The joy of the heart cannot be compared to any other joy. It is the joy we hear in the sound of babies and children laughing. It is the joy we feel when we seem to fly even though our feet are touching the ground. It is the joy we feel when we connect with the joy of others and it makes us grow inside. It is the joy we feel when we look around us in awe at the beauty of our planet, or when we look at the stars and have the sensation we are on one of them. The warmth and light of the sun gives us the joy of life, and the coolness of the moon makes us dream of going back home one day.

We all have that joy in our hearts. We were born with it and it is still here within us. Those who by negligence, distraction, weakness, forgetfulness or lack of asking for help have lost sight of it let us tell them that they still have it. They may have buried it in layers of other things, but that joy is intact waiting for the moment to be acknowledged.

The joy of the heart connects easily with all nature. If at sea, surrounded by water, our heart's joy joins the immensity of the sea and they become one. The joy is immense too. When we are in the snow and all we can see is white, we experience that joy as well. On a clear night in certain parts of the world when we can see the bright stars clearly, when they seem to be so big and close to us that we feel we could reach out and touch them, the joy bursts out in our hearts and it is beyond words. When we are on very high peaks and the view is breathtaking, we are connected. When we look into the eyes of another person and we seem to melt into one, we are connected. When we look into the shiny eyes of a beggar and see their depth, even though he is in a precarious situation he has not lost his joy, and we are at one with him too. A flower, a tree or a bush can make us feel exhilarating joy and connected to our hearts. The sounds of pleasant words with loving intonations, a loving gesture or a loving look all connect with us too. We could go on and on because from the moment we get up in the morning to the moment we go back to bed in the evening, if we are mindful of what we do and feel, we will be surprised how alive and connected the joy of our heart is.

There are many other joys that we may think are the real joy of our heart. It is important to know the difference. The joy from our heart is permanent whilst other joys are temporal.

The joy from the heart is present in all other joys and it is with the awareness we have of it that the joy can be felt with higher or lower sensations.

When we find the most sublime joy of the heart is when we meditate and we are absolutely connected to Source. We are Source. We just are. Any explanation of it would be inaccurate. One has to experience it for oneself. There are no words that would give a true account of how one feels. The only way to find out is by going there ourselves.

There has been too much fuss about meditation and some people think that it is difficult to do when, in fact, it is not. Meditation is the skill of doing nothing, wanting nothing, being nothing for the period of time we are meditating. At the beginning many thoughts bother us. If we do not engage with them, they will go away. In time our mind will learn to be silent and free from thoughts. Mantras can be used. We can find them in books or the internet. We can also make our own. Patience is a good ally. Start meditating for a few minutes and increase with time.

CELEBRATIONS

. . . .

Why do we choose to celebrate only some events in our lives? Why do we ignore others? For example, the fact we are breathing and through that we are alive in our chosen physical bodies. That calls for a constant celebration in our hearts. That is what is meant by celebration: having the heart full of joy and gratefulness.

There are celebrations where there are a lot of people and noise, alcohol and food, good intentions and glamour, but not the spark to light up the real joy of life on earth. It is sad to witness how people choose to be miserable when they have everything the heart could desire and they still find a tiny insignificant thing spoiling the celebration for them and for those around them. It only needs one person to sour the festive feeling in a celebration.

Rays of light emanate from people's grateful and joyful hearts and make the world a better place. They also make others feel great and everyone applauds their cheerfulness. They are always welcome. There is the laughter and joyfulness of children, with their excitement for celebrations and the enthusiasm they express for them, which shows how celebrations are meant to be. That is the spirit of celebrating life, which is the most precious thing we have. Celebrating what we have and being thankful for having it is being aware and awake.

When we recognise the challenges that life offers us in order to grow and learn how to expand our knowledge, when we accept them and feel blessed to have been chosen for those tasks, when we are grateful for such an honour, then we know who we are. We are projections of light that come with an aim to contribute to our universal immensity. Up to now, we have been forgetting this truth. We are now changing so rapidly that there is no time for that kind of dense light. We have been given a higher voltage to work with. However, as with all higher voltages, we have to be ready to receive its charge otherwise we will perish. Just as any machine we plug into the wrong voltage is ruined, we also are damaged and unable to function if the energy we receive is higher than we can cope with. This is why it is so important to be awake to this reality, because it will affect the believers and the non-believers. It has nothing to do with believing. The changes are happening already.

Those with higher vibration energies can feel the changes and how they accelerate as the days go by. The ones who are still sleeping do not notice anything going on, and yet everything is moving towards the big change. What is important to know is that we are in the right place, wherever we are, because we chose to be there.

We want to celebrate when we see the sun in the sky giving us warmth, light and life. We want to celebrate our own life, its richness, and the kindness with which Mother Earth takes care of us. We want to celebrate the ever-present beauty in every way possible on our magical planet. We want to celebrate all the other beings that chose to be here at the same time as us. We want to celebrate every instant of our time in the physical world, because we know it is temporary and can finish at any time, and we want to go back to the non-physical without regrets. We want to be able to celebrate the fact that what we came to do we have done well.

We are thankful to Source for having chosen us to experience this particular project.

OUR BIRTHDAY

We celebrate our birthday with parties, presents and lots of people around. How many of us, when celebrating our birthday, think of the reality and meaning of this day?

A celebration is always a happy event. When we celebrate our birthday, we celebrate not only our arrival on the planet, but also the fact we have managed to get here and are having the opportunity to clear so much out of our previous lives. We were able to come here to remove layers and layers of other time lines. We came with the intention of finding joy in everything, no matter what, because our nature is joy, love, light and infinity. However, we do not need to wait a whole year to celebrate the event of our birth: we can do it any other time as well. For instance, we can celebrate it in our heart every day at sunrise and sunset. We do not need to make a fuss about it. We can incorporate it into our daily practices.

How many of you remember arriving in this world? How many of you remember the world you came from? How many of you are longing to go back? How many of you are so attached to the physical body that the thought of parting from it terrifies you? How many of you think this world is the real world? How many of you know or remember the real world? How many of you are aware of other worlds? How many of you remember the programme we came with? And how many of you are following it? How many of you make sure you spend your birthday with your parents, thanking them once more for having welcomed you into their family?

We tend to forget that we are visitors on this planet and that we came with a very specific purpose. We tend to forget that our time here is limited to the time it takes to achieve our targets, and then we go back home. When we are aware of that we take advantage of our gift of being here. We often hear how those with terminal illnesses enjoy life to the fullest and their joy overflows in everything they do, because they know their time is limited and therefore precious. They have taken on board the fact of being alive with all the possibilities at hand and they use them well. We have heard from some of these people, that the only problem they had was the relatives or people around them, because of their attitude towards them and how they felt. This was making their transition difficult.

Let us celebrate for as many years as we have left. Let us be aware that those years are precious and let us make the most of them while we can. Let us make sure we do not waste time feeling sorry for ourselves or on trivial things. Let us be kind to others and especially ourselves, love others and ourselves and help and honour others and ourselves. Let us celebrate with awareness the love, light and joy of what we are. Let us feel the celebration of that joy and love every day of every year, with its overflow into everything we think, say and do.

Let us celebrate that our weaknesses transform into strengths, our ignorance into knowledge, our sleepiness into wakening, our dullness into joy and enthusiasm, and let it all be for the higher good of all. This present moment encompasses all the present moments of the past and future, and we want to thank Source for this celebration today.

BEING JUDGEMENTAL

People, with some exceptions, are judgemental. We judge others, situations, countries and ourselves. Why? What do we find or feel in doing it?

As observers we see that there seems to be something in some people that is triggered without them realising it and results in them judging and criticising others and also themselves. This is due to low self-esteem. It creates an uncomfortable feeling. They cannot understand the level at which others function. They cannot reach the standards they are judging others by. They feel frustrated by their own shortcomings. They feel envious of what others do, and yet they may not be aware of it. If there is something they do not understand, they judge it as either not being true or not being officially recognised. Their criteria are based on their low self-esteem, which does not allow them to see clearly. It is impossible to have a conversation with these people outside their limited world, because they will argue with you, denying whatever the subject is about. They will make assumptions about what it is or could be according to their limited knowledge. If contradicted, they become argumentative and the flavour of the conversation turns bitter. It is wise to move away from the topic before arriving at that point, otherwise we will find ourselves on the defensive and not reaching anywhere of interest for anyone.

For other people, it is ego that triggers their need to judge or criticise others. Ego can take them along many paths. It can be because they feel superior. We see this a lot. It can be out of ignorance or fear. However, being mindful is essential for us, because if we catch ourselves judging those who are judging others, that will be an indicator that we need to clear out our own judgement.

People judge in others what they do themselves. This can be seen when politicians accuse the opposing party of things they might do themselves. This is also found in the professional world and all around us. The most damaging judgement we can make is towards ourselves. If we judge ourselves, it is a sign of lack of love, honour and appreciation for who we are. It could also be a problem of low self-esteem. Whatever it is, it has to be dealt with without delay.

When judging others, we are judging ourselves. When we are criticising others, we are criticising ourselves. So what are we going to do about it? It could be of great help to us if, when we judge others or ourselves, we stop for a moment and look inside ourselves with compassion to see what triggers that judgemental feeling. Once we have found it, we proceed to deal with it. We use the tools we have or search for new ones. They will come to us easily. It is a wonderful feeling when we can remove blockages that are blinding us to the beauty of the world. Once we treat ourselves with love, respect, honour and appreciation of who we are, then we will be able to see others in the same way.

Bringing awareness regularly to who we are, where we are and what we are feeling will keep us in check and in our centre. The more we do it, the easier it becomes.

Before judging others, it would be a good idea to check where inside ourselves we have that which we are judging in others. If we could be free from that, we would not have judgemental ideas in our mind.

OPENING OUR MIND TO THE UNKNOWN

Opening our mind to the unknown allows the universe to expose us to the wonders of creation. It is our biggest adventure. Many people find it frightening, but those who dare to open up to it can only talk about wonders of beauty and wellbeing.

We have reached a time where more and more people are exploring unknown worlds. Some of them connect easily with beings from other stars and planets who pass on information about how we can evolve in many areas of our world. This is happening very rapidly now. There is more interest among the population for knowledge about these unknown worlds and their inhabitants.

There have been many accounts from those who have had contact with extra-terrestrial beings and there seem to be many differences between those accounts, which leaves us wondering if they came from different planets with different aims. There are many thousands of people living on planet earth who, through reincarnation or other ways, have come to help us evolve and help the planet on its way to the big change that is taking place. From what some of them say, we have always had help from other worlds in our universe. Terrestrials have tried to go to the moon and other places in the universe in search of life and other ways of living. By contrast, extra-terrestrials know how we live and what they can find in our planet. There may be the ones who want to take advantage of our weaknesses, but there are thousands of them helping us to ascend to a better way of living. They are in the best places to be effective in their objectives. If we are observant and sensitive to energies, we can spot them in many different jobs through the scale of society. There is something very special about these people: their presence, the way they speak, the way they act. They live with us. They seem to be like us but they are ahead of us.

They help us in many ways. Some people are sensitive to that help and some are not. However, the help is there for all of us. This may sound far-fetched for those with no interest beyond the limits of what they know. Nevertheless, the fact that they are not interested in the subject does not stop it from being true. When we close the doors to the unknown, what happens? We are stuck in our limitations of what we already know. Without this interest, what is new? How far can we advance in the sciences? What else can we invent electronically to make our lives easier? We would not have computers, robots, cars that drive themselves and so many other things.

Opening our minds to the unknown is inviting our helpers to show us new things, new ways, new expansions, new levels to aim for and reach in our own time.

There are those who have moved beyond help and can do it themselves. They know who they are and how to use the power we carry within us.

Meditation is the key to moving forward into knowledge. If we have knowledge, then fear of the unknown dissolves and we can be ourselves, our true selves.

Opening our minds to the unknown is looking at our life without limits, without restrictions.

REGRETS

. . . .

Most of us have or have had regrets of one kind or another, small and large. What causes us to regret? What are the consequences of our regrets? Can we do something about it?

Many of our regrets can lead us to feel guilt as well. Both combined make an unpleasant concoction, resulting in the body manifesting it in different kinds of ill health.

People regret thoughts they had, judgements they made, words they said or did not say, actions they took or did not take, behaviours they had or did not have, and all that can still be going on, even though they know there is an element of regret in it. The reasons for feeling regret have gained ground and become habits that can prove difficult to remove. Most people will keep thinking about their regrets or just retain them in their memory. This creates imbalances and ailments in the body.

Regrets keep people in chains and are blockages that stop them from being free, keeping them tied to the past.

Taking people and things for granted can lead to regrets later on. When loved ones pass on to the other side, we feel heart-broken. The memory searches the past, but having a negative tendency it will bring up the things we regret. When we do not take advantage of opportunities we have at hand, whether emotional, financial, practical or general, later on the regrets come. When we abuse our body with food and drink and the discomfort becomes painful, we regret having gone too far. Whatever the regret is about, it is in the past and the best thing we can do is learn the lesson and let go so it does not happen again.

When we have regrets, it is always about a judgement we make about having done wrong in the past. We are judging and punishing ourselves. It is as if by becoming aware of the harm we may have caused, our hearts feel the impact of it all and realise how it could have been avoided. It is painful to be in that situation and it also manifests that whatever we do to others we do to ourselves. Often what we say or do is based on anger, tiredness, jealousy, selfishness, unkindness or lack of self-esteem. Checking our reasons will help us eliminate situations that could bring us regrets.

When we follow our inner guidance, our heart is clear. We are calm and true to ourselves. We are honest and loving, and there is no place for conduct that will give us cause for regret.

We can easily dissolve blockages from the past or present that are preventing us from having a life of complete joy. Our awareness of how we feel and how we can deal with our feelings will be our pointers to how we find joy.

Loving ourselves and being aware is essential. Having a high self-esteem is helpful. Having compassion for the rest of creation is natural in us, if we allow it. Keeping up with learning and growing within is exciting. Being compassionate is in our nature.

OUR THOUGHTS

We think our thoughts are ours, but they are not always ours. Thoughts are energies with many different frequencies, which we can use for everything we wish. It is through our thoughts that our life takes shape and evolves. All our actions and manifestations start with thoughts.

It is hard to believe that those things we dislike tremendously or those that make us suffer could be the product of our own thoughts. That is why so many people blame others for it. It is beyond their comprehension that they would want to bring those things into their lives. Nevertheless, this is what has been happening, is happening now and will be happening in the future. When we take the time to look into ourselves attentively and observe the ins and outs of our actions and behaviour, we will be more than amazed at what we find.

Our lives are manifestations of thoughts and our perception of this from a terrestrial viewpoint is inconceivable. However, that is the truth of it. If we were to take any of our actions and trace them back to their origins, we would find the thought that gave them life. The only drawback is that we think and then forget we have thought. Once we have launched our thoughts, which are like orders we ask the universe to deliver, our unawareness of the fact stops us from seeing this happening. It works exactly like placing an order in a shop. The delivery will depend on what the item is, where it has to come from, and the shop we place our order in. We could say that our thoughts are orders placed in the universe and the delivery depends on the order and how many things we asked for at the same time, how it is sent and the power of vibration it has. So some things will happen instantly and others will take days or years, even different life times.

When we think the same thing over and over again, it becomes a habit and the habit can become a belief. This can have varied outcomes. It can be beneficial or detrimental to us. In any case we are stuck in our beliefs and there is no flexibility to accept anything new to move on in time. Then we pass on these beliefs to future generations and lead them to believe that is the way, thus creating a chain of beliefs that we may have picked up from a previous generation. We create programmes and conditions that we pass on as our ancestors passed them on to us. However, we have reached a time in our lives when we have to remove from ourselves all the programming and conditioning thrown at us on our arrival and throughout our lives.

The mind is a factory of thoughts. There are so many coming in and going out. A lot of them are not ours. Sometimes they are chaotic and entangled and we may not realise that we are dealing with thoughts that are not ours. Thoughts are persistent when we pay attention to them, when we engage with them or when we reject them. If we ignore them, they go. We can stop thoughts by observing them, not engaging with them, and through knowledge.

Through meditation we can remove all the programming and conditioning of the past. We can silence the mind in order to give it a rest and feel refreshed afterwards. We are calmer, the mind is still, and our thoughts are fewer and steadier and lead us to where we want to go. We become aware of them and what they can bring to us, so we choose what we think. Our lives change completely. We become strong and know how to face the challenges we may encounter. We go beyond the limitations imposed upon us and we know we are powerful beings. Our knowledge and guidance will serve us well and will lead us to see the limitless world in front of us with equally limitless opportunities to explore, experience and enjoy. The choice is ours.

BEING PRESENT

. . . .

We are absent a lot of the time and we do not even realise it. We notice when others in our company are absent and we feel uncomfortable about it. This is a sign that we are not this physical body we think we are, because if the mind is somewhere else the body is not reacting to what is being said or done. The senses seem to stop functioning.

Have you ever been with someone and had this awkward feeling that he or she was like an empty vessel, but when you bring their attention to the present, they react and come back to their body? A good observer can see and feel the difference. The most common cases we see are absent-minded people. They can be with us but thinking of something else, so their behaviour changes. They are in their thoughts and whatever is happening around their physical body is irrelevant to them because they are somewhere else. Our physical body is indeed like a vessel. If we are not in it, it does not respond. When we are not in our vessel we do not hear or see what is going on around us. Though our body is present, we are not. Have you experienced talking to someone who is not hearing you? The vessel is empty. Have you heard these expressions: "I didn't hear it", "you didn't tell me", "when did that happen? I don't recall it", and other similar ones? Have you been reading a book and suddenly you realise you have missed the information from the last few pages and you have to go back and read them again? Or have you been driving on a road and all of sudden you feel lost as if you have never been on that road, although it is the one you take every day to work? We are absent. Our presence is missing. It is disturbing when it happens to us. However, it shows us that the physical body would not be able to function by itself. It needs us to be in it.

When we are present, our presence stands out and we always know what to do. We have been in very difficult situations in various countries and our presence knew exactly what to do. Some people know by instinct because we all have that knowledge within us and it will come out by default to save the situation. Other people know it intellectually but do not know how to put it into practice, and that creates a resistance that prevents our natural automatic instinct from triggering.

When we are present, we are exempt from fear or any other negative feeling. We are natural, without ego dictating to us. We just are.

When we are present, our awareness is powerful because we are our true selves. All the masks we use in this physical world fall off and we are left with the presence of the Self.

Checking regularly if we are present or absent and taking the necessary measures to come to our centre in order to direct our life to our original program is what keeps us in harmony with ourselves and the world at large.

LOOSE BLOCKAGES IN US

No matter how much we know and how far we can reach there will always be loose blockages that will need fixing. When we start on our path we clear so much and we advance so noticeably that we think we have cleared it all, only to find we are still at the beginning of our journey. We were missing the point. The journey that takes us to our target is the pleasure of life itself. Once we arrive there is no more to do, so we go back home and start again.

What do we mean by loose blockages? They are blockages of energy moving loosely around. They can be debris from clearing energies, debris we pick up, debris we create ourselves and also the debris that is sent to us. We receive a lot of unwanted energies from those we consider friends or acquaintances, even from family. These blockages can be in the same fixed place bothering us or they can move around. Once we spot them, they have to be removed. There are ways and tools to do this.

We meet people who come to us because of a pain they cannot get rid of. They have been to doctors, they have taken medication prescribed to them, and yet the pain still persists. That kind of pain does not go away with medication, because it is a blockage of energy and has to be dissolved by energy.

Western society has to see the doctor for every little thing when the remedy is within them. Doctors used to reject anything that was not modern medicine. Nowadays there are more and more doctors who understand there are other ways of healing that are safer than medicines. There are some who recommend other ways of healing and they themselves practise it. We have met pharmacists on healing courses who have told us that they were worried about so many people constantly returning for repeat prescriptions. Some patients do so for years, and when asked if they felt better the answer is always "no". These pharmacists wanted to know if there was another way. They felt curious. They cared for those clients they had seen suffering for so long with no change. We felt great respect for them. They went out of their comfort zone to find out what was best for these clients.

With new technology medicine has advanced tremendously and we are all happy for that. However, there is a lot to say about prevention through nutrition, physical exercise, the life we lead and our spiritual practices.

When we look inside ourselves for information on how to deal with our own vexations and pains, we find the answers to deal with them. Silencing the mind will make it easier to go within ourselves. Meditation, of course, is the best tool. However, sitting quietly and allowing the mind to rest on a peaceful and pleasant thought will take us there. By just following the breath in and out will give us that gap of silence to be receptive and allow the answers to come in.

By being aware of our physical, emotional and mental body we are in a position of knowing what to do with energies that do not fit in and are not ours. That way we can fix those loose pieces in us.

WHEN THE TIME IS RIGHT

. . . .

We all want things instantly. We may be influenced by the speed of changes that take place so rapidly and by the technology we are surrounded with. There is so much more around us that helps us to advance rapidly in so many ways. However, there are certain things that advance at their own pace and we cannot speed them up in any other way.

Our thoughts take us to our desires, which in turn give intensity to our thoughts and to our vibration network in carrying out the actions needed to manifest our desires.

When we wake up from the illusory world we live in, we may feel overwhelmed. Each of us is different, and although we are on the same path we have dissimilar experiences. Some of us are quicker at picking up knowledge and applying it immediately. Others take longer. It could be due to the way they were brought up or how much desire is in them to follow the new path. There is also the baggage we carry from our past experiences. That includes past lives.

When our minds lead us to enquire and go within to find our true selves and wake up from the illusion we are living, we may find it hard to start with, because everything we were taught is contradicted by reality. We can be confused. If we do not have anyone to turn to or learn from, we may feel very lost at times. Fortunately these days there is information wherever we turn. The only difficulty is to find that which suits us and is appropriate for our personality. One thing we are sure of is that when we want something very much the universe will find ways to deliver it to us. Even without help and just trusting our inner power and awakening our dormant knowledge we will be aware of our true Self.

There are those who find the path easy because of their previous experiences in past time lines. The opposite is true for the same reason. There are also sceptics who will be thinking "all that is rubbish". There are also groups from the different religions who are still asleep and believe a saviour is coming to save them. The saviour is in their hearts waiting to be acknowledged.

In order to be steady in our awakening, it is necessary to be free from fears, anger, hate, jealousy, envy and other negative emotions we may have. To remove them is easy. The difficulty is how attached we are to them. There are many tools to work with and also many experts to help us, should we not feel up to doing it ourselves, although this is the most empowering thing to do.

When we hear the awakening call, we want things to happen to us quickly. They are happening but we cannot see them yet. Everything is happening constantly. We need to be awakened to see it. For that, we need patience and trust in ourselves, believing that we are that part of the Divine and we keep that divinity in our hearts. It has been within us all the time. That is our true Self. That is who we are.

When the time is right for us, we will understand everything without too many explanations.

GRATITUDE

. . . .

The power of being sincerely grateful matches the power of being in love. It is that deep. When we are very grateful, we are in that place where love resides.

We have seen miracles of gratefulness and how nature responds to us in order to convey feelings of gratitude. In honour of those moments we would like to mention a few:

There was a mother who was so grateful that her 16 year old son achieved an A grade in a GCSE exam, when he had failed in all other subjects, that she presented the teacher who had taught him that subject with a beautiful orchid. She could hardly speak from the emotion and shed tears of gratitude. That orchid flowered ceaselessly for twelve consecutive years and was the admiration of all who saw it.

There was a young woman who had a beautiful rose on her working desk at home. The rose was such an inspiration to her that she felt great gratitude towards it. Every day when she sat at her desk she felt grateful to the rose and begged it not to die. Three weeks had gone by and the rose was as fresh as the first day. The woman was surprised and had this idea: "What if the rose grew roots? It could live on for a long time". She started to wish through her love for the rose that this would happen. One day when she was changing the rose's water the woman saw that there were roots coming out. She was in awe. The rose had produced roots and stayed alive.

People have different ways of showing gratitude, but their eyes are always truthful. Through the work we do we have found many people who have expressed their gratefulness in very touching ways.

There was a very old, sick man who bent down to touch our feet because his emotion of gratefulness prevented him from speaking. The simple touch of his hand on our feet, even though we had shoes on, conveyed his emotion through our body all the way up to our head and we felt at one with him through the emotion of gratefulness.

We have items made by people out of gratefulness, and when they presented them to us they always said something that implied that those items did not reflect the magnitude of the power of gratitude they felt. Words were not necessary because their eyes were speaking the language of the heart, which was full of gratefulness - in other words, unconditional love.

What are you grateful for? What are we grateful for? We are grateful to our breath for keeping us alive. We are grateful to the sun, the moon, the stars and the whole universe. We are grateful to Mother Earth for our body and for providing for all our needs in the physical world. We are grateful to our parents for bringing us up and taking care of us. We are grateful for the gift of being parents ourselves. We are grateful for everything, and to everyone who makes our life possible, from the highest scientists who create the latest technology to the street sweepers who keep our streets clean. In short, we are grateful to the whole collective, whatever their role is in this present life we happen to share. Without their input we would not exist as we do at this time.

To us it is important to keep gratefulness alive at all times because each breath is a gift, each smile we give or receive is a gift. A kind word, help we ask for, the sun and the rain are all gifts not to be taken for granted; nor should our family and friends or anyone else be. We are all where we are supposed to be, doing what we are supposed to do, and therefore cooperating with the universal expansion of which we are part and very grateful for.

THE ROLE OF PARENTS

Most parents do their best to bring their children up. It all depends on how they see life and where they stand financially, culturally and geographically. Whatever situations parents are in, they will always use their resources to help their children to do well in life. But there are always exceptions.

Children, before they come to our planet, search carefully for the parents who will give them the best conditions for the role they want to play in the physical world. The role of the parents is to take care of them while they are growing up and help them with their basic needs. They can pass on their knowledge of life and their wisdom but cannot impose on them what they are going to be, because children already come with a programme and it is up to them to follow it. When parents interfere too much, they make it very difficult for their children. Some children will feel quite strongly what they want to do, but others will not and they will become confused and struggle.

The best parents can do is learn from their children, observe, stand by and let them develop. Children come with new ideas. They know more than their parents about what the future holds for them. So they need to be free to act on their ideas.

Parents suffer unnecessarily because of the great love they feel for their children. It is good to remember that children come with baggage, which they need to experience and remove. They may need your support, but on the other side of the coin, they may have come to help you deal with whatever issues you may have. Everything is happening for a very definite reason.

We hear constantly of the miraculous words children utter, their actions, the amazing knowledge they have, how gifted they are at the age of two and all the way up. Have you asked yourself: Why? Where does that knowledge come from? What does it mean? Are these children here to wake up their parents and the world?

When we are grateful for our children, our heart feels joy and unconditional love flows easily, free from attachments or wanting to control. It is good to remember that children are gifts from God, and in the same way they came to their parents they can also be taken from them. Parents think that their children belong to them. This is an illusion. Children are just visitors for a period of time until they can manage for themselves. They are not possessions anyone can have. They are the force of life in its expansion.

The best parents are those who treat their children as the best gifts they could ever have. They honour and respect them. They help them in this physical world without removing anything they may bring from other worlds. They guide and support them without imposing on them or controlling them. They are open to new ideas they may bring. They are aware that these lovely children are with them for a temporary period of time and have their own journey to deal with. They take advantage of being together, and make the most of it with the knowledge that they are equals and they are helping each other, even though they may not be aware of it. The best thing you can do for your children is LOVE them UNCONDITIONALLY every day of your life.

OUR HEALTH

· ·

Our health is very much talked about nowadays and many people come up with new ideas, diets and remedies. No doubt all that is helpful, but it does not always solve our problems.

Our ill health is telling us something we are ignoring and as soon as we pay attention and make changes the problems will go. Sometimes it is not so easy, mainly because we do not know what is wrong or how to go about making it better. So we go to see a doctor, who will look into our case and may find what the problem is. From there on, depending on the illness found, there could be many visits to doctors and hospitals, as well as many medicines to take; and many other things may happen. That is all fine and we are grateful to the doctors and medical staff. However, there are easier and quicker ways to solve some health problems, and at less cost.

We have to understand that our body is an amazing piece of work. It has everything necessary to function well. Our physical body is the vehicle we have to travel in through this physical world; it has been made to perfection for us. If we are in tune with it and listen to what it communicates to us, we will always know what to do to be healthy. Our body is the best source of information we have. It can tell us when things go wrong or go well. It is up to us to know our body well, be sensitive, listen and pay attention to it. That will help the world to be a healthier place.

When the body complains, it is attracting our attention to the fact that something is not well. If we respect and honour our body, we stop there and then, and assess the situation. What is wrong? What is happening? What are our thoughts? How are we feeling? Where are we? These are some of the questions whose answers will guide us to where the problem is. As stated above, it may be something easily solved by making changes.

When we have other problems we do not think we can tackle ourselves, it is alright to go and see a doctor. However, bear in mind that doctors deal with symptoms and not with the root of the problem in the majority of cases. The symptoms may change and doctors will change the prescriptions. We are still patients and the problem has not been solved. There are many problems modern medicine cannot heal - as many healers or herbalists can testify.

There are, however, ways to heal easily even though the methods are not tangible to the naked eye. Our body is made out of trillions of cells. Those cells are energy; therefore, we can heal through energy. We cannot see it, but some of us can feel it. The energy that can cause ill health does not have to be from this present life. It can be from past lives and we are ready now to change it. This means that we can sometimes heal ourselves. We have to remember that a healer can guide us and help us, but we are the ones who can heal ourselves. We are our own healers.

Many cases of ill health are caused by our thoughts. We have a long list of examples that were easily solved by the people involved changing their thoughts. A healthy mind has a healthy body and vice versa.

We frequently find de-motivated people feeling tired, low in self-esteem, with pains in different parts of the body and other aches. All this is the body giving signals that something is not going well and asking us to stop and find out what it is. Then we do something to remedy it. If you need help from someone else, allow your heart to guide you to the right person, who will help you to find yourself rather than becoming dependant on him or her.

Let it be known that there is always a reason for whatever we do. If we abuse our body through food, drink or exhaustion of any kind, we can find out what drives us to those extremes and, if we do not know how to do it, let us find some help.

Fear and anger are damaging to our wellbeing. We only have to remember that they are energies and we can change them into those that can help us to be healthy.

It is important to remember that our health is in OUR hands. It is up to us to be healthy. It is our responsibility to be healthy and not that of doctors or medical services. They can be of help but the responsibility remains ours.

A joyful heart and smiling face are great contributions to our wellbeing. Let us respect, honour and love our body, for it is precious in many ways and irreplaceable in this time line.

FREEDOM

· ·

Freedom is an overused word and is often used without much sense. What is freedom? It depends on our understanding of it. There are many interpretations and, if asked, each of us would give a different definition.

Incarcerated prisoners have more freedom than many walking the streets. Unfortunately, there are many people who become prisoners in themselves. Their prison can be more suffocating than penitentiaries. The results of this can create anxiety, illness, depression, anger, fear, worry and other problems. This comes from a lack of knowing who they are and refusing to find out.

As soon as we realise that freedom comes from within and not from without, as soon as it becomes clear to us that freedom does not come from the material world but from the inner world, and as soon as we remove our misconceptions of what freedom is, we will start tasting it. Then, we will be experiencing a sense of liberation of our inner being.

A free person is one who has a clear conscience and a peaceful mind. Our mind can imprison us if we allow it. The mind finds ways to trap us into thinking negatively. It is up to us to be alert and mindful of what goes through our mind and address it before it is bigger than us. Our firm intentions play a considerable role and can be supported by the precious tool we carry with us at all times: our breath. When the mind insists on taking us where we do not want to go we can control it through our breath. There are many techniques we can use for this. If you do not know them, you can simply have the intention that you want to and focus your attention on your breath, feeling it coming in and out. Make it slow and comfortable and think of nothing else but your breath. Very soon, your sensations will be speaking to you and you will become aware of a deeper being within you. The sensations will intensify and you will have reached a way of appeasing the mind.

When things go wrong for us the tendency is to blame circumstances, others, the job, the government or anything else. It would help us all, if we became aware that we are our own co-creators and whatever happens to us, we have created it. The fact that either we ignore this or we have forgotten about it does not change anything. Whatever we project with our thoughts and words will come to us, maybe in ways we do not recognise, but they are still our own.

It is painful to see people harming one another or criticising one another because they are so blind that they cannot see they are doing it to themselves and to the whole of creation, since we are all one. The arrogance that goes with ignorance is the most difficult to deal with.

When our mind is free, we can see more clearly. When our heart is free, we can love the world unconditionally. When we wish everyone to have the same happiness we wish for ourselves, we are taking care of ourselves and our planet. When all this dawns on us, we will be approaching freedom, and then it is up to us to allow it in to stay with us or not. The choice is always ours.

RELATIONSHIPS

· ·

Relationships are unique, as unique as we are ourselves, and cannot be compared because there will always be unseen details that will make a big difference to the comparison.

The relationship with our parents is the first one we experience. It can vary according to circumstances. It does not matter whether we are born into a rich or poor family. Let us focus here on the richness of love, because it is the only richness that will make a relationship work. We can see many differences within a family in the kind of relationship parents have with their children and later on with grandchildren, plus all the circle of relatives. We can move on to friends, who very often represent more than family in some people's lives. Each individual relationship is different to the other, even though they may seem similar and may be doing the same things.

The relationship between couples can range from being the easiest to the most difficult of them all. Each couple is a world of its own, and how some stay together and survive as couples is a mystery. One thing some couples have in common is that they are strangers to each other and they do not know it. They think they know each other well merely because they know their likes and dislikes and their behaviour in the physical world. However, they do not know the reasons for their meeting up, why they are together, why they cannot see things that would break up their relationship, and why small things do just that. If any partner from any relationship would open his or her heart with sincerity and say what they thought of the other, in most cases, it would not correspond to what the other one thought.

There is a greater intelligence that orchestrates encounters, whether they want it or not. They are not always aware. Even when time wears out the initial attraction and they start to see more clearly what they do not like in each other, the greater intelligence will hide from them what is obvious to others, and this will keep couples together. They are doing more than living together. They are healing the past.

Many years ago now, we used to know a German girl. She was beautiful, elegant, well educated and with a good job. She knew an English boy, who was the opposite. He was smaller than her, shabby, not good looking, not educated and his job was of no consequence and therefore he did not earn a lot of money. The boy liked the girl and knew where she worked, so he would be around when she was passing by. The girl used to tell us he got on her nerves and used to make unkind comments about him. One day when we were coming out of work, the boy was waiting for her. She waved at him with a smile. We asked if they had become friends and she said they were going out together. With shock we reminded her of all the things she used to say about him. Her answer was that she knew all that and she could still see all those things in him, but now she really wanted to be with him and have his children.

If we look from the outside we will see couples who do not seem to match at all. Yet they must be well suited, but this cannot be seen through the eyes of terrestrials.

If a relationship becomes difficult and you want to get out of it, but somehow your heart is telling you to hold on, even though everyone else is saying the opposite, it would pay in the long run to follow the heart. It is in the heart we keep the knowledge of the physical and non-physical worlds. There are always options to look into the relationship and make it work.

SILENCE

· ·

The most beautiful silence is the silence of the mind. When the mind is silent we have the opportunity of renewing ourselves, refreshing our lives, re-energising our system, creating new projects, living in the present moment, being aware and mindful of our surroundings and being a useful tool to our planet and the collective.

Silencing the mind may seem an easy thing to do until we put ourselves to the task. Then we can appreciate what a great job those who meditate for hours do. We mention meditation here in the real sense of meditation: having the mind free from any thoughts or desires in this physical world. Those who meditate know how revitalising and refreshing it is to have the mind at rest for a period of time daily. It changes people's lives.

We live in a world of noises. Everywhere we go there is noise. We are transported by noises. With so much noise around us, we cannot hear ourselves. We are drowned by noises and people turn the volume up on their gadgets as if they could not hear otherwise. This obsession for loudness creates addiction and makes it difficult for people to be silent. They need the noises. On one of our courses a man told us:

"I don't remember ever not having noises around me. At work there are noises all the time, and I couldn't be without noises at home. I always used to have the radio on, no matter what I did or where I was in the house. The radio was on and I carried it around with me. I didn't listen to it most of the time, but I couldn't bear the silence. Now, doing these exercises I don't have the radio on. I don't need it and I feel different. It's like a big change in my life. It's as if I'm a new person and feel different. I love it. I never knew I could feel this good. Now, I can relax. I couldn't before. When I come home from work, I can be in my own company and I enjoy it".

Are you suffering from the same noise addiction? Do you need your phone with you to play games, watch films or programmes, listen to music or other things all the time? When you are not at work or, in some cases even at work, do you check you mind frequently? How does it feel? Agitated?

Busy? Frustrated? Angry? Calm? It is well known that an over-burdened mind can be affected by depression and negativity. There are many tools to deal with these situations. There are also many professionals who will happily guide you.

When people go on holiday there are still more noises, because of the crowds on the beaches, in restaurants or wherever they go. So where to go to find silence? Silent retreats can be very good if they are well organised. However, there are rules and lectures involved, which suit the majority of people but not some of us. Places can be found around the world where we can have silence. Once we have found physical silence, then we can hear how noisy and loud our mind is. A lot of people need help to calm the mind. Our personality and our needs will be the pointers to what we are looking for. Research on retreats will avoid disappointments.

Having the mind occupied all the time creates stress. Silence will give it a break and keep it well balanced. That way life will run smoothly and enhance the states mentioned above.

On the road to silence the mind can lead us to knowledge, to waking up to who we are, to communicating with awareness with our true Self. All that will benefit us and the whole planet.

ENJOYING THE COMPANY OF THE HIGHER SELF

Enjoying the company of the higher Self. What do we mean by that? Isn't our higher Self with us all the time?

That is right. Our higher Self is with us all the time, whether we believe it or not, whether we notice it or not, whether we pay attention to it or ignore it. Without our higher Self our physical body would not exist. It is good to bear in mind that it is not our body that succumbs to death, but our higher Self that leaves the body behind when it is time to go. So we do not die. We move on. Our body acts as a transport vessel and as a means to provide us with the experiences of the senses. It is as temporary as the first bicycle we had or the first car we drove. They were good. They gave us pleasure and learning, but we moved on in life to better things.

Not many of us have the patience required to deal with life in the very diverse and complicated cases it presents to us. We do not have it when dealing with people, no matter what the circumstances may be. Our patience runs out when we are tired, selfish, angry, arrogant and so on. Patience also runs out waiting in queues or waiting-rooms.

On the other hand, we have very patient and loving people. They take care of everyone and everything around them: people, animals, plants, anything. They are carers and are moved by unconditional love. There are others who are kind but lack patience. However, they are ready to be of help at any time.

There are those who know better. They use their waiting time to enjoy their higher Self. Why waste such precious time when it can be used for such a joy as communicating with the Self? It has bonuses too, because it gives them a pause in their programme of the day. By being in full awareness of the self and grateful for the moment they will feel enriched and fulfilled.

By taking life, people and the planet for granted we are missing the essence of what is worth having. By being so busy with triviality, we miss the important things in our life. By being vague about what we are supposed to do, we do not see our priorities. By being negligent, we make a lot of errors. By defending ourselves with excuses, we are not taking responsibility for our actions. Allowing ourselves to make good use of what would be wasted time gives us a chance to focus on our higher Self and that in itself is as beneficial as it can get in every possible way.

When we enjoy the company of the higher Self, we also enjoy the wellbeing of the whole planet and the collective. We see it all as one. There are no partitions or divisions. We are one and work as one. It is alright if there are some of you who do not understand this concept. It will come back to you when you are ready to receive it and understand it. We remember well, years ago, when we read a book and there was a paragraph that we agreed with but could not make ours. Now it is fully with us. We often think of it. Time and place are vital for us to accommodate knowledge and action. Patience and good use of waiting time is too.

Our higher Self is with us at all times. Awareness brings it to our present when we allow it.

EVERYTHING AND NOTHING

. . . .

When we ponder everything and nothing, we have one foot on each side and we do not know which to choose. We still have to go on learning to find out which would suit us best. If in everything there is abundance, why are we wondering? If in nothing everything is lacking, why are we stuck? We are indecisive because we have not found the combination that merges the two. Just like a coin, they each have a side but they are one piece. They exist together and are valued as one.

We can have everything we put our mind to. There are no limits and the earth has presented us with the most amazing display of things we can choose from. Everyone is eligible to choose from the great exhibition the planet offers us. There is abundance everywhere we look, yet we do not feel satisfied. We feel something is missing.

There are some people who cannot see the abundance. They do not see anything at all and lock themselves in the chambers of lacking. Some will be wrapped up in "poor me" mode and others will be dreaming of a better life. They are also missing a part of themselves, even if they are not aware what it is. In both situations we are not quite hitting the right equation, because they are separate from each other and it is in the union that we become our real true selves.

When we become aware that everything and nothing are one and all the rest is an illusion, then our life changes. We can see our behaviour with different eyes and feel the impact of our knowledge. We become aware of the games we play, how we play them and where we choose to play them. We watch carefully how they develop and affect others and ourselves. We become observers and players at the same time. Being aware puts us in a different seat from where we can see the show better. Now we are in a position to enjoy all we do without reservations.

We are feeling better with our discovery now. However, we have another issue to overcome. How to live among those who have not awakened to the same knowledge as us? What seems to us the most natural thing, they find incomprehensible or a touch mad. As is always the case when embracing ignorance, it does not matter who knocks at the door; it will be defended strongly. We just accept it as part of the game and those players play the way they know how. That should not stop us from adjusting to them. But at the same time we follow our inner guidance to be able to manage our energies so as to work with both sides of the coin. There will come a time when they will also want to exit the old paradigm and make haste to reach the new one.

Our heart will be letting us know whether we are on the right path or not. Our energies will vibrate according to what we think, say or do. We are always co-creating our life.

We are everything, everyone and nothing at the same time. If this does not feel right for you now, that is fine. You are not ready or you do not wish to be ready for this yet.

ENTHUSIASM

. . . .

Enthusiasm is the force of life driven by our inner universal energy. It has the power to do and undo everything. All we need is to feel and vibrate that enthusiasm within us and feel great with it, feel confident with the knowing conviction that everything is possible.

If we observe children they can give us lessons in enthusiasm. They have it bubbling around and in them at play, when they ask their parents for something they want, when they get it and enjoy it. They feel creative and talk about their way of making it happen. They look at life in their own way and talk about it. As we listen to them we get drawn into their story and they make us feel as if it is happening. So we are born with enthusiasm. We cannot complain that we do not have it. We may have it hidden by layers of other things, and we need to dig to reach it. It is there somewhere within us for sure. What can we do? Look for it. Remove the layers that are obstructing it and use it to its full capacity.

This natural enthusiasm is contagious. When we are in the presence of people who have other attributes to complement their enthusiasm we feel a magnetic attraction towards them. They draw us to them. They have something powerful, which we can identify within ourselves too. This is the time to ask ourselves: are we using this powerful source of energy or are we suffocating it? It does not matter what we do or what profession we are in, enthusiasm always works to our benefit and that of those around us and beyond.

Sometimes we see people who misuse the gift of enthusiasm so that they are the only beneficiaries. We are mindful about such people and withdraw from their company or business. And that is alright. We do not have to judge them. That is what they do. We do not have to cooperate with them or engage with them. Should we be in a situation where we are with them and cannot avoid it, we would have to use our skills and tools to get out of it.

It is most important at all times to know who we are and what we stand for. This will help us to have a clear idea of the path we want to follow and the circles we want to move in, so we do not waste time trying out other people's ideas. We are always learning. From good examples we can add to our ideas, and from bad ones we make sure we do not fall into those pits.

Enthusiasm, when backed up with intelligence, trust, kindness and coherence, can create amazing achievements. The best way to prove it is by trying it ourselves.

Do you ask yourself questions such as: How do I feel? Do I feel grumpy? Miserable? Pitiful? Angry? Or, do I feel grateful? Happy? Enthusiastic? Energetic? Kind? Loving? Compassionate?

Why am I feeling this way? If it is a good feeling, celebrate it. If it is a bad one, what can you do about it? There are always reasons for the way we feel and there are equally always ways of moving on. Help is available; we just have to want it. If we do not ask for it, we may never have it offered to us. Nobody can help us but ourselves. However, we can get guidance and support.

One thing is important to remember: our enthusiasm is power. We can use it all the time with everyone, including ourselves. We can never run out of it. It is our nature. It is our life force.

SIGNPOSTS

When we are awake the Universal Intelligence, Source of All Creation, uses many ways to communicate with us. It gives us clues with signposts. They are tailor-made, so we will get whatever we are most likely to understand. The clues are within us too. Our physical body gives us clues constantly, but not all of us are aware of them.

When people have a gut feeling, what do they do? Usually, if they ignore it they will regret it later. But if they act on it they will obtain good results.

Several people have told us that when they were doing something that they were not supposed to, alarm bells rang in their heads telling them not to do it. Others said they heard someone telling them not to go ahead. They ignored it and ended up in prison. All of them had somewhat different warnings but they all said: "I could have avoided this, if I had listened to what I was hearing". They had the choice. They could have chosen. Some do not feel or hear anything. Some are not awake enough and others are still sleeping.

People are attracted to a particular thing at a particular time in their lives that suddenly appears in front of them and has a meaning for them. It all depends on their expectations, their hopes, their feelings, their thoughts, their dreams and the projects they are working on. To them those unexpected items or sights or anything else have a meaning and purpose for them to move one way or another. Here their gut feeling plays a role as well as directing them to make the right choice. Some people have a strong feeling that is pulling them into something that is bigger than them. Even though they may feel in deep water at times, they still carry on. The force that is pushing them to the limits is showing them that there are no limits. If you look around, you will find many examples. Here are a couple of examples of signposts:

A young man, very worried and with no help to hand, was lying in bed and could not sleep. Through the window he saw a bright star shining with a powerful light, outshining the other stars. His heart was lifted as if it had been injected with life and the hope that everything was going to be fine. He relaxed and went to sleep. The events that followed all went well.

A woman was going to a meeting knowing what the meeting was going to be about. On the way there she saw a tiny object on the floor that attracted her attention. She stopped, picked it up and paused for a few seconds allowing the information to come in. She felt in her heart that the meeting was going to be totally different to what she was expecting and she had to be prepared. This was very helpful, so when she arrived she knew what to do rather than reacting and spoiling the outcome of the meeting. Her intuition was correct and she was prepared, so the meeting went well.

Nature is very good at showing signposts, if we are close to it. Trees, bushes and flowers are good indicators for showing us our state of being and what it should be. They can also predict what states of mind are around the corner for us so we can be prepared. Pets are also good at that if you have a good relationship with them. They really know a lot about what is going on and if you can communicate with them there is much to be learned. Have you ever hurt yourself on the corner of a table? Knocked something over? Spilt your drink? If you immediately ask yourself: "What was in my mind?" You will have the answer to the incident. They are all signposts. Being aware of the Universe's signposts helps us to navigate through life mindfully.

EVERY CLOUD HAS A SILVER LINING

Many, if not all of us, feel unhappy about unpleasant incidents in our lives and in the lives of others around the world. We are connected and therefore we feel the hurt and pain in others. Our mind has a tendency to take us to the negative side of any situation. We are so immersed in the dark side of it that we do not see the real reason for the incident. However, all things have a cause and effect, even if we are not aware of it.

Have you ever been surprised by incidents that just occur for no apparent reason and you cannot work out what brought them up? You may feel lost wanting to comprehend what is happening and you may turn the problem around in your head many times looking for answers or reasons that could bring light into the situation. The more you think about it, the worse it gets, because you may be bringing baggage from the past and adding to it, thus complicating things. It is only when sitting down calmly that you review the whole situation and ask yourself questions about it. If your mind is clear of judgements, only then can you see why the incident happened. The more you open up, the more you see. You will reach a point where you can see the good side of the incident and how without it you would not have been able to discover hidden opportunities to move forward.

We never welcome situations that make us sad and struggle to get out of them. But when we turn it up side down the view is different. Then we can move towards greener fields with more scope and possibilities.

People enjoy telling stories that may have happened to them or their relatives, and they make such a big drama out of them that those listening feel burdened with the sad news. That leads them to retell the stories to someone else. In that way the stories get longer and longer, and everyone reinterprets them and retells them in their own way. So it is like an infection that is passed on and becomes out of hand. On the other hand, embracing the situation with mindfulness will help us take steps that will help others and ourselves to find the silver lining.

We may have periods in our lives when we are blocked by unresolved incidents. We also have other incidents from past time lines. These can bring many feelings that can vary from being depressed, tired, ill, frustrated, angry, and so on. If you feel that way, look for help. If what the doctor gives you does not work, look for other types of healing.

We do not have to live putting up with things that make us unhappy. There are solutions for everything. Sometimes people call them miracles, merely because they have never thought of them themselves and therefore did not believe them possible. Miracles happen daily for those who choose to see them. We have to be careful how we see others too.

We had heard that the husband of a young woman we knew had left her and they had just divorced. We met her and said how sorry we were about her situation. Her reply was that she was very happy to have got rid of him and now she was living with a man she loved.

So when we look at the bright side of whatever happens, we are moving forward.

Every cloud has a silver lining. If we do not see it, let us keep looking for it.

TO BE ACKNOWLEDGED

. . . .

We may go through our whole life not being aware how important it is to acknowledge others and be acknowledged by others. Everyone wants to have his or her work appreciated. That is a good incentive to do the work better. This applies to every job, profession and family.

When students are acknowledged for the effort they put into their work, their interest in studying will increase and they will excel. The reverse will be the case if they are ignored or criticised. Workers and professionals respond to acknowledgement in the same way. Treat them well, appreciate what they do, and they will do it better. Colleagues will be more willing to help out if they know it is going to be appreciated and reciprocated. Neighbours will do the same. At home, among members of the family is where it is most needed, because it is at home where we learn the codes of conduct. What we learn from our families we are going to take with us into the world. Of course there are always exceptions. However, a good base formed by respect and awareness of what everyone does is important so we can use it in our lives. Parenthood is not recognised as one of the most important professions and many problems in society come from that. Many parents do not know what they are doing and are unhappy about it. They feel trapped because they were not prepared for that huge responsibility.

When we are mindful we are in the present moment and in touch with what is around us. We react to it according to our perceptions of life and the respect we have for ourselves. We have all heard comments such as:

- *"What is the point? He will never appreciate it." "Why bother? He won't see it." "They think they are the only ones who work here."*
- *"I know I work extra hours, but I want to finish the job. They trust me and they treat me so well that I cannot let them down." "I stayed longer at work than I should, but I love my job and they appreciate what I do." "Working long hours doesn't bother me if I get acknowledgement for it."*

We were in a shop paying for an item and we complimented the cashier on the jewellery she was wearing. Her eyes watered as she thanked us. Then, as she was putting the item in a bag, she added. "You've made my day! So far it's been horrible. This is the first nice thing I've heard all day". We felt for her. By doing that, we were connected to her. It is so simple to make people feel good. Complements are like sparks that light up hearts that are being crushed.

We were talking to a young woman about how proud her parents were of her, and she said: "if they are so proud, why don't they acknowledge me instead of ignoring me when I come full of excitement to tell them I have been promoted or have succeeded in a difficult project? I need their acknowledgement then and not a month later. They have no idea how discouraging and painful that is".

We wrote to someone well known. He replied in person rather than through his secretary, and that made us feel good. We felt connected and acknowledged.

It is important to acknowledge what is around us in whatever way it presents itself.

FREE THE SOUL FROM WITHIN

We have talked about freedom and detachment, baggage we carry from the past and the programming we are subjected to by parents and society. We have talked about the expansion of our presence on planet earth, our vibration mechanisms and the subtle ways we receive information from our true Self. We have talked about changes, but changes are happening all the time. What we mean is big changes that we have never seen before and are taking place, even though they are not visible to those who sleep or do not want to see.

In the physical world changes are happening at a speed that is hard for us to keep up with. New different and faster technology keeps appearing in the market and is keeping us on our toes to be up to date with it. Even so, we still do not know everything and keep discovering new inventions if we look for them.

In the energy world everything moves faster, and although it is not tangible, we can see the changes taking place in seconds, when it used to take weeks, months, years or decades. Awakening to the light has made people more receptive and through their various experiences they open up much more than they have in the past.

Now we are facing much bigger changes in every possible way. What can we do? If we are still sleeping we can wake and seek information. We are entering a new era, a new world. The important thing is to be aware of what is happening and not dismiss it as if it were not going to affect us, because it will. Knowledge and preparation will make the changes easier.

Those who are awake are prepared or preparing and are already merging into the energies they want to be in. Everyone is welcome to join. It is never too late if you are prepared to change your mind.

Masaru Emoto could see how we poison water with our thoughts and feelings. He lectured around the world informing and warning people about it. He wrote books on the subject. We heard him saying in an interview that water would be a problem in the future if people did not change their ways. If you have never seen his photos, they are an eye opener to what we do with our minds, thoughts and feelings. We can make things rotten and ugly and we can make them healthy and beautiful. Masaru Emoto worked with water. We are mostly water. The planet is mostly water. The water of the planet is in danger and it is up to us to save it by sending loving and appreciative thoughts to it every day.

Our soul has been stuck within us for too long. All those ideas we may have about beliefs, traditions and ways of doing things are simply programmes that have enchained us to keep us the slaves of others. The time has come to change all that. Now the tune is different. There will be those who will follow the new tune and be free or who will stay with the old tune and remain in the old paradigm. Regardless of the choice we make, being prepared will help.

Being free from within is the real freedom. The light makes us ascend to glorious ways of living and opens the doors to an existence of love and wellbeing not experienced before on earth. Changes are inevitable, but the choice is ours. In all cases, preparations are needed.

THE NEWS

. . . .

There are people who listen to the news as if it were the most important thing of the day. There are others who will not bother with the news on the basis that it is always the same: tragedies, disasters, factories closing down, unemployment, etc. It rarely covers other things. Amazing people are doing amazing things, and yet the news only concentrates on the bad things. The audience feels awful after hearing or watching the news. But guess what? It does not stop there. The news will be the principal topic of conversation among the population. In other words, it is continually passing negativity around and increasing its volume as it passes from person to person, group to group, community to community, country to country. That creates negative feelings in people, especially fear.

How about having a "Bad News Channel" and a "Good News Channel"?

There are so many programmes specialising in how to bring wellbeing to people. However, we have not seen anyone who checks the effects caused on those who watch the news every day. Doctors keep saying how negative feelings create chronic diseases and the government creates programmes to deal with them. It is interesting that with so many experts around, the news has not been found to be one of the causes that affects those illnesses.

We hear people saying that they have to read the newspaper every day as a priority. Others will listen to the radio or watch TV with the same interest. There is nothing wrong with that. The only thing is that the news tends to inform on the negative side of life and there is so much more to say about the positive side, which is rarely covered. If it were, that would enhance the positive side in people.

Many professionals will agree that if we feed our mind with negative information, it will have a negative effect on our body. Unfortunately, it will end up as diseases.

If you were one of those who want a clear mind and a healthy body, what would you do? What would you recommend?

The food we eat can make us healthy or ill. In the same way, the food we feed our mind can also make us healthy or ill. Our responsibility is to take care of the good health of both mind and body.

There is a lot of information on the internet about our physical, mental and emotional health. By checking how we are feeling we will know what to do. Delaying it will not make it go away.

We all have the power to heal ourselves. Sometimes we lack information. The good thing is that these days in our electronic world we have it at our fingertips. Choosing the information we take in will affect the state of health of our mind and body.

WHAT ARE WE LOOKING FOR?

What are you looking for? A better job? A better house? A better hobby? Better friends? A better life altogether? Is it to satisfy the nagging feeling of dissatisfaction within? How are you going about finding those things? Or are you not looking for anything at all?

The majority of people worry a lot about their day-to-day life. They go from task to task or enjoyment to enjoyment and are satisfied with that. Their vision is limited. Others go further because they know there is more to be discovered. They look up and see there are worlds around us and they want to know them. So they busy themselves finding out about them. There are many others already engaged in interplanetary communications with fabulous information to share. There are those who have lost their way but keep dreaming of finding it one day. There are the gurus or wise ones who have knowledge to impart. There are also those who find themselves in remote places without the advantages of teachers present, but they use nature as their teacher and the planet as their school. They learn to go within in silence and allow the answers to come through. Which are you?

The physical world is full of distractions and activities. Everyone is running round satisfying their interests, so there is not enough time to stop and check if their health is well and if they are happy and smiling from the heart. Then one day the body complains with aches and pains indicating that something has to be done. Then, sometimes, it is too late.

Many things are taken for granted, especially the planet and nature. Deforestation does not seem to matter to the majority, nor the extinction of species either. The generosity of Mother Earth, in giving us everything we can possibly need, has been abused for a long time. The damage we are doing will have an effect on generations to come. Where do you find yourself in this problematic situation?

We have a physical body which has all it needs to be healthy. We just need to look after it with care and love. It is most important that we know our body, how it functions, and that it can heal itself under the right conditions by eating the right foods, drinking sufficient water and having the appropriate rest. Our body is our best friend and our best source of information for letting us know when something is wrong. Mindfulness will help. Do you take care of your body?

Our physical body responds to our thoughts and feelings. If we feel pain, in a foot, elbow or any other part of the body, this is a warning for us. Most people run to the doctor. In fact, all it may be is a thought that persists or a strong feeling about something like fear or guilt. Any negative feeling can produce an effect on the body, which will respond with a physical ache somewhere. If it is not dealt with, it can end up as an illness. We have to remember that anything we put in our body through our mind, we can also remove with our mind. We do not need to go to the doctor. We can do it ourselves. We all have the power and knowledge to do it. Some people may have forgotten about it. To bring it back, they may need some guidance by a professional who deals with natural healing.

Remember that all the answers are within us. We can find them in inner silence.

PRAYER OR MEDITATION

• •

What is prayer? What is meditation? Why do we pray or meditate? Some people pray every day as a duty, a self-imposed duty. Their performance is like that of robots. There is no feeling. They have great respect for the one they may be praying to but that is all. Why are we praying? Is it out of fear or ignorance? There could be many reasons. We pray to deities to ask for something, to thank them for something, to save our soul, to honour them, or out of fear when we are in chaos or in a tragedy. We meditate to find clarity of mind as to which path to take and what choices to make. We also meditate to honour our higher Self, to seek enlightenment, and to rest in the Self.

Prayer and meditation are similar, with the difference that meditation is a higher way of praying. We can reach our God in any way we choose, because our God is with us at all times. There is no need to go to any special place to be with the Highest Being, since it is everywhere at all times. However, we have to point out that where people gather to pray, there is a powerful energy, which can be felt mostly and more strongly when we find the location empty or semi-empty. When there are multitudes, the energy is not the same. Maybe not everyone is there to pray, or their prayers are not so devoted as they need be to create the energy of love and belonging that emanates from the Divine.

Do you pray? In what way do you pray? Is your prayer asking for personal things or wellbeing for all? Do you meditate? What are your reasons? What do you get out of it?

Praying or meditating is an act of intimacy with the Self. It is powerful, very powerful and we have to take care how we go into it, so we get the best results. For most of us, all we want is to be connected to the Divine. For that we do not need temples or churches; we can do it wherever we happen to be. Of course it will be easier in the silence of a church or temple, because they are sacred places, rather than in a supermarket, a street or a noisy house. If we are in nature, we can find everything we need. That is the best temple. Nevertheless, in nature there are also different energies and we have to choose our spot with awareness. Our intuition will let us know the difference through how we feel about the place. Being on top of a high mountain is exhilarating and peaceful at the same time. We can also find a special spot for us to be in silence in a corner of our garden, public gardens, parks, rivers or the sea. However, the best temple is our physical body. It does not matter where we find ourselves. This is one of the reasons we treat our body well, care for it, and respect it in every way. It is our sanctuary for the Divine within.

No matter where we pray or meditate, the important thing is to do it. It makes us feel good to be connected to our Source of wellbeing. We are careful about what we ask for and what our intentions are so as to obtain results that will benefit us all.

We pray or meditate when we communicate in silence with our Inner Source of wellbeing.

ANCHORS AND AGREEMENTS

. . . .

Throughout our life we continually throw anchors out to latch onto moments of our experiences. The reasons for it can vary from happy to unhappy ones. The fact is that we hold on to these anchors without considering the damage they cause us through the limitations that they inflict on us.

How do we find them? There are probably many ways. Past anchors can be disguised to appear different according to the interpretation each of us understands best. For example, let us imagine you have certain principles in the way you see and want to live your life, but you find yourself resisting those principles. In other words, you find yourself doing the opposite of what you would like to do, and even though you may feel uncomfortable doing it, you continue doing it for a long time without realising it. Then one day it hits you. You can see it clearly. It is then you start looking for ways to remove whatever is preventing you from living your life as you desire; in other words, living without resistances or inclinations to go another way. It is then you discover the anchors stopping you from doing what you want.

For some of us, the way it works is through mindfulness. Knowing and observing ourselves helps tremendously. Observing how we feel at all times, honouring our feelings by paying attention, and questioning the reasons for their existence will lead us to these anchors. We have to bear in mind that sometimes it can be very subtle and it takes insights to reach them. Other times, we may resist following our feelings because we sense that it could be painful, so we avoid them. By avoiding them we perpetuate the obstructions caused by them, and that does not help us to move forward into the next dimension.

When we find ourselves in situations where we are thinking, speaking or doing what does not make us happy, because it does not match the vibration of how we want to feel or how we want our life to be, then it is time to question the reasons for it. The danger here is to find superficial excuses. If we want to be true to ourselves, we will go deeper into how we feel and how that matches what is happening. By taking a few moments of silence from within, asking the necessary questions and with the right intentions, we can balance the imbalances we may have.

Anchors can also be agreements we made with ourselves or with others which seemed to make sense when they were made but are now out of date. In other words, they do not serve us any longer. We may not be aware of them and if we are, we may treat them as a thing of the past that we do not think about anymore. Nevertheless, they are alive and obstructing our journey, stopping us from moving forward.

Do you know? We can be so loaded with intangible burdens that unless someone guides us to uncover them, we could be missing great opportunities in our life just because our unawareness of the heavy weights we carry prevents us from seeing them.

Everything is as easy or difficult as we want it to be. Everything that we find in our way we have put there ourselves and we have the knowledge to remove it in the same way. It is up to us.

STRETCHING OURSELVES TOO MUCH

e live in a fast-moving world, which frequently propels us to stretch ourselves more than our physical body can cope with. When we become aware of this, we have crossed the line that keeps us safe. Does this happen to you? If it does, what do you do? Do you change your ways? Do you ask for help? Do you ask for support? What are your options?

What we have noticed as we progress through this digital world is that people, instead of having more free time, seem to work more hours. This is because companies are growing faster and their expansion requires more manpower, which can involve some people giving more hours of their own time. They may feel stimulated with the challenges the job offers and with their involvement in the never-ending new ways of managing those challenges. They are caught in a network of progress. A word of caution: What are the consequences in their personal lives? Recently someone told us: "I am so into my work that I don't see anything else. Something happened in my life and I was shocked to realised that I had lost my sense of emotions and hadn't noticed".

One does not have to work for a company: one can be a mother taking care of her family, a working single parent, a volunteer, and so on. People who engage themselves in doing too much are driven by their desire for satisfaction and feelings of accomplishment. Being mindful of how we affect those around us, and its consequences, will keep us aware of how far we can go so we can stop before it is too late. The issues could relate to health, relationships, family life, social life, etc.

The most important thing is our health and wellbeing at all levels: physical, emotional and mental. When this is the case all the other things in our life work well if mindfulness is present. However, if we stretch ourselves too much we are putting ourselves in a vulnerable situation that can get out of control. Have you noticed that when you have been over-stretched your mind works slower, you lose focus, become irritable and lose patience easily; you make mistakes which you would not normally make, say the wrong thing, and so on?

Have you noticed if your nutrition and sleep are balanced?

If planetary energies are moving faster, it is normal that we follow suit, even though we may not be aware we do. This calls for reflection on our part and a stop on our busy path to ask ourselves questions - about ourselves, the people we live with, the earth we live on, the universe we are part of and how a combination of all these makes us what we are. Giving ourselves time for reflection will make us more aware of our lives and how we live. We will feel more complete and satisfied, and without regrets.

Stretching ourselves more than is good for us can fool us into being great achievers in the short term. But long-term results have a price that we cannot always afford to pay. The right food, rest, physical exercise, and a clear mind, together with meditation and awareness, will help us to be in our centre and enjoy life to the fullest.

A NOTE TO THE READERS

Thank you for reading this book whether you read it out of interest, curiosity, help or any other reason. I hope you are enjoying reading it as much as I enjoyed writing it. The same vibrational energy that pushed me to write it has guided you to find it and want to read it. I suggest you keep this book in an accessible place for you to pick it up at any time you may find yourself in a state of mind that needs a reminder of who we all are.

Your comments will be welcome and appreciated at:

hello@adelitabroom.com
www.adelitabroom.com
www.facebook.com/awakeningtoyourself/

ACKNOWLEDGEMENTS

I would like to thank my husband, David, and my daughter, Annabel, for the proofreading and helpful comments. Thanks also to my son, Daniel, for all his encouragement and support.